AWAKEN YOUR *Inner* DIAMOND

CREATE THE SUSTAINABLE BUSINESS YOU'VE BEEN CHASING AND LIVE IN ALIGNMENT WITHOUT SACRIFICING WHO YOU ARE

ANGELA TSAI

AWAKEN YOUR INNER DIAMOND / Angela Tsai /

ISBN 978-969-5792-26-1

Published in UK by GYBWI, a traded brand by MOX Ventures LTD.

https://www.growyourbrandwithimpact.com/

Cover design & typesetting by Isse & X. Shan

Disclaimer: This publication is designed to provide information regarding the subject matter covered based on the authors' subjective experience. It is sold with the understanding that the publisher and authors are not engaged in rendering any healthcare, financial advice, or other professional services. If you require healthcare advice or other expert assistance, you should seek the services of a licensed professional. The publisher and authors assume no responsibility for errors, inconsistencies, or omissions. Additionally, client names and identifying details have been changed to protect individual privacy. Neither is any liability assumed for damages resulting from the use of the information contained herein

This is a letter of self-love.

To help the **secretly doubting high achievers make their story and impact.** By awakening their true extraordinariness and reconnecting with who they are. So they can trust themselves to go after their dream. Without feeling storyless, disconnected, or unfulfilled.

Underlying themes: Love, Leadership, Courage

The roadmap to truly going for it, and making it.

Unlocked through the One-Page VISION.

DEDICATIONS

For my daughter. To know that she can have it all. The career. The life. The family. The dream. Without sacrificing freedom or losing who she is.

For YOU, dear reader. You are the bold one. And the inspiration for me to share these stories.

Know that no matter where you are today, you already have the courage in you for the way forward. May this be the dose of encouragement needed to further your pursuit of the bold dreams you are bravely going after.

TABLE OF CONTENTS

PRELUDE

This book is written to serve as a practical guide.

Either to be read from beginning to end—or jump straight to the chapter that will most speak to what you need emotionally and mentally right now.

A LETTER OF LOVE,
DEAR READER:

You are stronger than you feel right now.

You are infinitely stronger.

Those in your life and those whom you have touched,

they are better because of you.

Stay focused on your lane. You are incomparable. You are your own unique person.

You are fierce, intense, serious, and a force.

You inspire.

Look only at what you can do, and those you can help, those that will be attracted to your style and your vibe.

Be 100% you.

Anyone who makes you feel bad, doubt yourself, or feel unworthy, ditch them.

Keep around you only the ones that make you feel like you can take over the world.

Those that make you feel like you are bloody fantastic.

Because that is the true you.

And don't compare yourself to others.

Whatever you have to handle right now, or do,

Or whatever you have set in your sights to achieve—

You've got it.

Angela Tsai

INTRODUCTION – THE CALLING NORMAL LIFE, THEN.

So, what is my story?

Perhaps the start of my story is no story at all? How sad would that be. That there was no story to begin. I feel trapped in my past, and it prevents me from living.

As I asked myself the questions, the crazy idea suddenly came up in my mind: *What if I just go?* Take a sabbatical. Take off work for a few months, and figure out my soul. Now, looking back, it is actually crazy to think just how ludicrous that idea seemed to me at the time. *What do you mean you want to take three months off work? Are you lazy?*

Today, as a business owner running a business based on a model of 16 hours a week, balanced with being a mum to my two-year-old—my headspace is completely different. But at the time, it was another story. What followed was three months of the most liberating and free moments in my life up until then. Free traveling through South America without any agenda or itinerary.

On a whim I could book a flight in two days to head to Galapagos. Or jump on a bus, and then cross the border by foot over to Bolivia.

Meeting and traveling with characters from all walks of life. A Korean son of a publisher. A Canadian ex-Microsoft programmer on his second year of travel, who sold all his belongings and bought a motorcycle and rode his way down to South America. A young Dutch student just finished with her exchange programme in Peru and getting through her travels before returning home. And countless other stories of wanderlusters and high-achieving professionals just like me who had either paused their career to travel, or were otherwise seeking to awaken something deeper inside them for a little while.

My plan at the time was that I would give myself three months of clarity, then return to my fast-paced career and life.

Because what else was there, right?

But it is always through the unexpected moments of chaos—followed by shock… then stillness—that clarity suddenly comes. It happened, for me, because all the unimportant stuff that I thought mattered and that I cared about was suddenly stripped away and disappeared. Until I could only focus on and deal with the situation at hand.

My leap out of my corporate career path and into business was not one that I chose. It took having the carpet ripped from under my feet and suddenly having to depend on others for that shift to happen.

I wonder, when was that moment of calling for you?

Then.

I vividly remember the moment I got the call from my boss. "Congratulations, you got accepted into the programme." She was referring to a prestigious leadership programme at one of the world's most esteemed organisations that I was working for at the time. I remember a C-level friend of mine in the tech startup space had told me he knew about the programme. And I thought to myself, well, if outsiders knew about it, it must be notoriously high quality and top of the top!

Life was very work-centred then.

I lived the fast-paced lifestyle. Working long hours, the crushing daily London underground commute on the northern line. Getting in the office early to down another double espresso and settling into the deal room for another day of battling and brainstorming to grow our market and win deals. There was no reason to expect that this would ever change.

In my final months before I chose to leave that life, I helped bring in over $120 million in revenue through new portfolios into the marketing services business unit I was responsible for expanding in the UK.

The programme offered a months-long experience where teams competed against each other, culminating in a week in Chicago to pitch the next big strategy idea to a panel of judges—an opportunity to take this billion-dollar empire to the next level. The organisation invested hundreds of thousands of dollars in this world-class training to build their next wave of leaders. For a company of half a million people—all smart, bright, and ambitious—being selected for this programme was a big deal.

I was in Australia and in my dad's living room.

I mean, this is an honour, right? Who says 'no' to this opportunity? But is it really what I want?

I wasn't excited. *How ungrateful,* I thought immediately.

There wasn't any big bang event, but a series of events that shook me and made me think. There was the moment I heard the news of a colleague dying on a business trip of a heart attack. He must have been in his forties. Then there was watching a presentation by our CEO—at that time terminally ill—talking about bringing more humanness into our workplace, as he focused on spending time with his family. There were the multiple signs of my own exhaustion and emotional burnout, which turned into complete disconnection, that I ignored over the years.

Is this my life? I thought. *I work, I work, I work… and then I die?*

The lack of sleep where five hours a night was considered normal. Tension and guilt from Mum that I wasn't calling her enough—*how can she not understand that I already have so much on my plate?* The difficulty in properly connecting and holding down romantic relationships. The constant feeling of guilt for not being there enough for friends and family. Constantly feeling like I was letting people down. Calling up my best friend in Australia at 2 a.m. in tears. Not actually knowing why I was in tears or feeling so bad.

There was the moment I was sitting and staring blankly at the laptop screen in the office. About to enter a presentation that my team member had secured with the CEO, followed by another pitch that afternoon in front of an executive marketing team. Staring at the screen blankly and my head going numb.

In Japan, the word *karoshi* means the condition of dying of overwork. At least there, there is an acknowledgement of the unhealthiness of such a lifestyle.

Is this really my purpose?

Work-centred people have a drive to work.

Unhealthy habits and chronic anxiety and stress was a norm. Running at a fast pace and proud of it. It was a badge of honour to be so busy. To be so *needed*.

When you are in it, it is hard to see a way out. I reached a point where I was simply no longer excited at the prospect of continuing. 2 a.m. at the office working on a deal we had been pushing to close for the last three months. Exhausted and forcing my brain to stay switched on. I thought to myself, *I have not been working till the 2-3 a.m. finishes every single night, skipping weekends, to lose this deal.* And with that came a new surge of strength. Sometime during this pitch, my girlfriend messaged me. "You ARE coming tonight, right? You know that this is important to me." It was her partner's birthday.

I had an 8 p.m. bid meeting that night. With discomfort, I knew I couldn't skip it. The birthday, that is.

And I thought to myself, *where have my priorities gone?*

It was a moment when I realised something needed to change.

There are these conversations you have with yourself that stick with you. Glass balls versus bouncy balls. Take care of the glass balls in your life. The bouncy ones—work, for example—will always come back.

When the new job I was due to start when I returned to London suddenly fell through due to an error by immigration lawyers responsible for transferring my employer sponsorship visa (normally a routine thing), I was suddenly barred from entry back into London, and then deported back to Australia with no clear road to return. I suddenly had to figure out how to start again from scratch. It took several more months before I decided to give up that life for good.

The corporate world sets up walls—both the physical and visible… and the invisible, created by the boundaries of the social layer within.

"Oh, you shouldn't put that on your LinkedIn, that might upset people."

"You need to get close to this person, keep them on your side."

It's a world that has so much defined me, I felt safe with the rigidity of the constraints. I always knew how to climb and be successful within it… but my potential never felt close to being filled. Jumping into business was a beautiful taste of freedom, which was great until the reality hit that this wasn't a vacation. And you actually have to make money from this to make it viable.

And such was the beginning of a new journey to find myself.

It took me a long time again to realise that the answer all the time, and holding me back from success, was all in my head. The baggage from my corporate days. The worrying and concern about others' judgment and the lack of real self-belief. All hidden behind a wall of 'fake it till you make it' confidence that revealed its true face once all the titles and status was stripped away.

Over the years I have spent tens of thousands on business and marketing coaching through all kinds of gurus and mentors. But the mindset journey was by far the toughest, beyond all the strategy in the world. Through this book, I'm excited to share with you all I have learnt to help you on your own journey.

This is about the ability to rewire, rediscover, and reconnect to the core identity that is already in each of us—and then trusting yourself to move forward. You simply need to re-find him/her.

The sole purpose of this book is to help the **secretly doubting high achievers everywhere to make their story and impact**. By awakening their true extraordinariness (inner diamond) within and reconnecting with who they are. So they can trust themselves to go after their dream. Without feeling storyless, disconnected, or unfulfilled.

PART ONE

YOUR IMPACT

1

THE UNRAVELLING

The journey starts here. Go from feeling like just a cog in a wheel to knowing that you have significance and a greater story already inside you. (I believe in you)

❖ The beginning

Sitting in the holding room in Heathrow. It was slowly sinking in what was happening — but I wasn't believing it.

Moments before, I was text messaging with my best friend, who had driven to the airport to meet me.

"Haha," she joked, "they must think you're a drug mule."

It was a cold, bright, empty, large space with rows of blue plastic chairs, enclosed by a door locked from the outside. Large glass window panes through which we could be observed. The clock on the wall showed

8:45 a.m. There was a single payphone in the corner. A water cooler with white plastic cups.

If we needed food, we could knock on the glass window, and someone would warm up one of these convenience pack meals for us in the microwave. In the corner there was an older woman in cloaks, lying down on a mattress — it looked like she had been there for a while, perhaps a couple of days. In front of me there was a young blond girl, softly crying.

How did this happen? How did I get here?

I had all my identity documents taken, and my personal belongings put into a locked room separated from the holding space I was in. And a decision that would impact my entire life was now in the hands of a border officer who told me to stay put. With no indication of how long it was actually going to take.

"Everything is going to be fine," I told myself. A sort of numbness was setting in. Pushing away the sinking realisation of what may happen, my brain was on high alert and already running through the multiple scenarios and next steps.

But let me rewind a bit.

I was fresh off a 19-hour flight from Argentina back to London. Returning after a 3-month travel sabbatical—initially meant as time away to clear my head and reset, but it turned out instead to be an in-between-jobs break. During my 15 years living as an 'expat' on employer-sponsored visas in Europe, it had never felt like a necessity to obtain citizenship. Looking back, I definitely think the expat status

ANGELA TSAI

gave me a sense of importance in the value of 'me' as an employee, and a sort of prestige.

How silly now, looking back. But no different to all those external badges of validation we often use to claim our value (rather than looking internally).

"I'm getting headhunted."

"They're promoting me to X."

"Work is SO busy, I just can't get away."

Salaries. Titles. Being needed. Feeling 'wanted'.

In the Netherlands, which is where I began my expat career, the term for expats is *kennismigrant*. It means 'knowledge workers'—workers that are in demand because of the skills that we bring. But this dependence on the external validation also turned out to be my personal downfall.

Despite all the due diligence I had done on my own part with my own lawyers checking the paperwork to ensure no gaps in the transition, the agency in charge of the transfer messed up. Missed a critical window for the paperwork to be submitted. And with that, with a click of the fingers, my residency was revoked.

I was about to be deported. With no chance of another corporate employer sponsoring me for 12 months. The new company I was due to start at washed their hands of the deal with the reasoning that "the offer was all conditional on the sponsorship transfer being successful."

Literally. Shit.

All the bubble wrapping and artificial safety I had created for myself unravelled in that moment.

The journey. Always starts somewhat the same. Something happens. It awakens a misalignment felt deep inside.

A calling… repeated. That we often ignore. Until you no longer can.

What happens when you lose it all?

Nothing is coincidence. And years later, I am forever grateful for that moment. Because without it, I likely would never have let go. Letting go, or being let go, rather, released me for the full freedom that I was about to discover.

Trusting myself, that I'm going to be okay. It is often these major life events and moments that shake us out of our comfort.

They are our moments of invitation to step towards our dream. How we respond to those moments, and what we fight for, determines whether it becomes the moment we let go and go for it, or stay in a place of artificial 'safety'.

❖ The real reasons behind feeling storyless and disconnected—aware or not

You know those moments. The fake it till you make it bravado. Sometimes you fake so well that you start to forget you are pretending. And then, before all those feelings have time to settle, when the uncomfortable prickles of self-doubt start to rise from within you— boom, you jump to the next thing.

A next promotion. A next project. A next honorary title or badge to add to the nonstop growing pile of accolades at your feet. Each a further branch of validation. A further armour that prevents you from confronting your inner truth. Addressing that growing emptiness from within. *Who am I? What is my value to the world?*

The more successful you are, the worse the self-doubt. And the more armour you then feel you need to add. A growing addiction. And the idea that if we dare to stop moving… dare to stop climbing… and dare to stop adding more achievements under our belt… we become immediately irrelevant. Such is the curse, and simultaneously the internal drive of FIRE, that you as the high achiever will know.

My theory is that most, if not all, high achievers are what I refer to as 'secretly doubting' high achievers. Even if they are unaware and this doubt lives only in their subconscious. Successful people are not necessarily high achievers (although many of them are). Yet not all high achievers will become successful people—at least, not in a way they will identify and recognise.

Perhaps this is you. Being driven by a deep fire within yourself, which you already know too well, comes with its light and with its shadow. Both of which, if we do not catch it, do not make ourselves aware of it, can swallow us whole in an instant.

Imagine what life would be like if your sense of value, worth, and success were no longer tied to your daily and lifetime achievements. The TED Talk. The published book. The business revenue goal reached. Each career milestone. All other significant milestones in your life.

Would you still be successful? Would you feel it? Would you believe it?

❖ Hiding in the big bold dark

When I look back at my career, I definitely think there were these moments where I knew I was hiding. I wonder if you recognise this for yourself? A sense of internal conflict. Even during the moments of highs. 'Successes' and leadership roles. Where I didn't show it.

The air in the room was thick with tension. The day on edge. An exhausted team worked to the brim of maximum energy exertion. It had been like this for weeks. Yet today—it could all be over in an instant, wiping away months of hard work, with about $10 million in revenue on the line. Thrown in the deep end. I had just taken over a challenging multi-pillar marketing deal that I was originally only meant to be running a small part of. Every action was under scrutiny. The client didn't want us there.

The client had been forced into the decision by top management for cost-cutting reasons. But he didn't want the change. His team didn't want the change. And that was clear. Our team were working hard, but it was getting harder and harder to keep them moralised. The deadline to decide whether to pull the plug was 5 p.m. The team had worked almost through the night to clear the backlog of issues and bring the project back to green.

Swaying this difficult client to come back onside while motivating discouraged team members through chaos, toxicity, and animosity on the ground, was definitely a key period I count among the most significant in my growth and career. It required all my tools (that at the time were very limited) as a new leader—to empower the team, and give safety and security. Taking full ownership of whatever came, and being the fall-back when things went wrong.

In the same period, I was being promoted into leadership positions. I experienced uncomfortable pushback and dismissive attitudes from senior male colleagues, who outranked me and refused to recognise or respect my authority.

Outwardly, I presented that I didn't care. That I was beyond the belittling behaviours aimed to put me back in my place. Inwardly, I knew I was holding everything back.

I was secretly crumbling and just barely holding on. Until the sleepless nights alone with my thoughts. Where my seeds of self-doubt would open and show their true, ugly face.

This disconnect in my professional identity manifested itself in my private relationships. The insecurities that I did not allow to surface at work, I allowed to take over there. I sought validation in those relationships, and in that handed over my personal power.

Those early years in my twenties and early thirties, when I was finding the grounding and centre within myself, were challenging ones. Walking the walk. Talking the talk. But certainly not feeling it.

One year, I discovered Amy Cuddy's TEDx talk 'Presence'. I took from it that no matter how I felt on the inside, I could always choose how I showed up. Elevating my external impact and results. But it came at a cost. Endless chasing of the next milestone or achievement—instead of truly looking inward. I still resonate with Amy's words; it's a great talk and one to check out for every person, and especially woman, seeking to conquer their inner beasts. But imagine the power of doing this transformation from both inside and out.

Not only faking it till you make it, but actually FEELING it.

Perhaps you recognise some of this within your own journey.

Superficial 'growth', and pushing through despite of it all, does not remove the internal doubts, conflicts, and fears that are manifesting and growing inside.

Yes, actions build confidence. But without getting to the root cause of disconnect with your own authenticity through awareness, it will continue to be a constant uphill battle. And a psychological, mental, emotional, and physical toll that eventually builds up like a pressure pot until we crack.

Creating a hard STOP—exactly in the moments we need to go. Burnout. Freeze. Paralysis.

We all have those moments. Where we allow the little voices and seeds of (un)truth to get to us. Over time, this builds and starts to become framed as reality in our heads. The feeling of not being good enough. The heavy weight of burden, obligation, and responsibility. That it's all somehow your fault that this isn't working.

That somehow things come easier to others than they do to you because of whatever limitation within yourself. Because you are not 'so and so', and it is all so much easier for them because…

The sources of these little voices are often external. But the truth is that most originate early on in our lives—far away from the context of now, in the moments when they show their ugly heads.

What we often do not realise is that voices come from all directions. Every day. Every moment. Negative and positive. It is how our brains are hardwired from early conditioning that determines the wavelengths we pick up and keep.

It determines how we interpret those voices, those words, and whether we accept them as true. It means that our inner dialogues and words are what is ACTUALLY creating the self-doubt we feel and the negative things we tell ourselves. The narratives and meanings that we have chosen (usually unconsciously) to give air to.

The good news is that it also means it is fully in our power—once we become aware of this—to choose the words and inner dialogues that empower us versus feed our doubt.

❖ Liz: The Intervention

Several years ago, I was at a self-development retreat in Bali, witnessing an intervention.

A woman, Liz (my roommate), was sharing her story of estrangement from her father, whom she and her brothers had not spoken to for 10 years. She recounted their unstable childhood.

"We were plucked like plants," she said, "and moved from country to country." This was due to their father's work.

I watched as Liz sought validation and empathy for the pain and trauma she and her brothers experienced. It was difficult to watch, because she was not receiving that, but rather a constant rebuttal and pushback—sometimes quite harshly—from the coach on stage.

He was pushing her to focus on facts, and not on the story and meaning that she had created her entire life. It was clear that this wasn't a therapy session for sympathy and healing emotional wounds. At least not in the traditional therapeutic sense. To be fair, it also wasn't what we were there for. The retreat's goal was to literally 'break' our inner critic. Break free of the stories that had been holding us back in our lives and business. And that it certainly did.

Being her roommate, I had the unique perspective to see how things unfolded after that. It was during this retreat that she worked up the courage to phone her dad. She wasn't even sure that the number she had would still work. Nor that he would answer the phone. But he did.

Afterwards, we talked. She told me she felt surprised by the conversation. He sounded old, she said. He had aged. He was different. He was so happy to hear from her—his only daughter.

Today, as a coach myself, such extreme methods are not ones I choose to employ. (My personal belief is that extreme methods like this, if not paired with the right level of empathy and support to follow, can create more damage or continue to mask what is at the root.)

However, it was illustrative of the power of our internal narratives and meanings, and how these can keep us trapped. For Liz, it was a narrative that had kept her relationship with her father locked in limbo for 10 years. She tried (unsuccessfully) to convince her brothers to do the same. They point-blank refused. But in her case, it was a relationship reopened.

Being a mother now myself has opened up so much for me to understand my own childhood. And to better understand the world from my parents' perspective.

Along with the experiences I've gained through my work, and the stories (mine and others) I shall be sharing in this book, it's opened up a different way of viewing the world and accessing a different perspective. One that empowers you forward, rather than becoming another reason you cannot. And that is what I hope to pass to you.

Stoicism philosophy teaches that you are already living the dream life—the difference is that the dream life is not yours. You are living the dream life of someone else.

In Liz's story, perhaps another person would have loved the opportunity to travel the world, to become worldly and international (which she was) as a result. She spoke multiple languages, which opened doors to opportunities through the people and places she was exposed to.

This doesn't take away from the experiences and feelings she had, but it was also what gave strength to the possibility and potentials unlocked within her as a person.

❖ There is a greater story inside you

Our stories matter.

And experiences are not relative. Experiences are beautiful, individual, and stand alone. Each in its own character.

Things only matter if you choose for them to. And thus the only reason that we will ever feel storyless and disconnected is because **we have created a story** telling ourselves as much.

We have placed a frame around our own story and experience. Often this is in relation to something external, or to someone else's story. And we decide that our own story is somehow less-than or doesn't matter as much. Isn't it ironic that the reason we often feel we don't have a story or feel disconnected with who we are… is exactly because of a story?

In learning to rewire and rewrite your own story, rather than allowing that false internal narrative to frame that story for you, you hold within you the power to release yourself.

Let's begin that rewriting process.

2

WHY YOU MUST UNCOVER YOUR STORY, AND WHY THE WORLD NEEDS IT

When our inner voice whispers, it's an urgent call to uncover your story and realign to living your truth. This is beyond just you; it extends to how you will make your contribution to the world. (The voice of urgency—"I must do this.")

❖ The fearless spear thrower

You have greatness in you. And an untold and untapped potential. More than you can imagine, beyond your wildest dreams.

Late in the 19th century, a young man was brought up in poverty—more the norm than the exception at the time. Son to a struggling artist and performer, he was 12 years old when he scored his first breakthrough. But the one thing that got him through those hard years in early childhood was an unwavering vision and belief.

"Even as I was fighting every day, for survival, finding basic needs to survive—I always believed I was the world's best actor."

That young boy was Charlie Chaplin.

And he is the perfect example of the power of inner narratives and how our beliefs shape and sustain our external outcomes. His empowering narrative began in childhood. But yours can begin at any moment you choose.

Chaplin had an innate and rather unique ability to fully see and feel his potential, what he was meant for, the contribution he was meant to make in the world. That unwavering vision enabled him to fearlessly throw himself out there, over and over. To experience the failures and ridicule.

(And isn't that what we are often so afraid of, when we venture and put ourselves out there in business?)

But this vision also enabled him to make the massive waves that forever changed the entertainment and film industry.

The fearless spear thrower within him. And you have one in you as well.

❖ Practical Section: Turning life's 'interruptions' into alignment with your true path

While Chaplin might have had a head start in understanding this for himself, **the only ingredients that you will need to understand this in your own life are:**

1. **The 'knowing' that there is more potential within you to uncap, and**

2. **Recognising 'the trigger' to realign towards your inner truth.**

This trigger will almost always come in the form of an interruption.

What do I mean by interruption? I mean some sort of event that throws you off the flow of continuing down the stream, forcing you to re-evaluate and question.

The choice for you at this point, then, is—do I listen to that interruption? Or find the next familiar stream?

When I first entered the world of business, I never believed it would be my forever path. I believed that this would be a fun playground time to dabble in experiencing some freedom until I was ready to re-enter the work world. It was meant to be simply an experience, a sort of extended sabbatical. And a space to express my creativity.

After my new job unexpectedly fell through and I was forced to return to Australia, it was the first time ever in my life that I had been forced to simply… be still.

And to reflect: What am I here for? What am I meant for? What is it that I want to do?

Tools appear in our life at the moments we need them most.

My sister had recently returned from a personal development workshop, and it was during the countless existential conversations we had during that forced extended time home that she passed this concept on to me. I later learnt it was called *Ikigai*.

To find the heart of what I was meant for.

Let's go through the questions:

- What are you good at (skills that you know you bring to the table with ease)?

- What are you appreciated for (by others)?

- What makes the world better (how you contribute to improving others and the environment)?

For me, I realised at the heart of this analysis was a single word—IMPACT.

Specifically, enabling others to make their impact.

What is yours?

> ***To access a free PDF download to guide you through this process, go to***
> ***https://growyourbrandwithimpact.com/self-reflection-gybwi***

This is a powerful exercise.

And from my experience having done this both for close family and friends, as well as clients, once you dig and discover the heart of this, you can never unsee it. You can never 'un-know' it.

Knowing, though, does not automatically lead to realisation. It took me many more years in business to fully understand what was really at the heart of it and to realise it in my execution.

What was I meant for? How is it 'valued'? And how am I uniquely meant to bring it to the world? Why was I continuously burning out and depleting myself? Or falling into comparison and doubt about whether it had all already been done before?

These are the existential questions that are at the exciting heart of discovery as you build this business.

And answering these questions has everything to do with that internal narrative we wrap around our stories—continuing to work through your previous hard-wirings.

❖ Practical Section: The essence of your real story

How do you tell your stories?

When it comes to our internal narratives, there is a spectrum that runs through every story that is told.

On one end of the spectrum are the stories that are pared down, played down, made to seem less than they are. And on the other end of the spectrum are stories that, well… do the opposite.

We've all experienced and told stories that fit into either of those moulds.

Reflecting on your own natural starting point—the way YOU tend to tell your stories—allows you to identify your current intrinsic sense of value to the world (from your perspective). It allows you to uncover the essence of your REAL story in a way that will authentically connect with others, allowing you to feel seen as the true you.

And to be able to start creating real, positive change that lasts in those you want to impact.

Exercise: Uncover the starting point of your own story

    i.   Run through the Ikigai exercise if you have not yet done for yourself. You can download a free template for this here: https://growyourbrandwithimpact.com/self-reflection-gybwi

    ii.   Deep down, do you believe that you have a story that matters and an impact to achieve? Or do you feel that you are relatively normal, nothing special, and who are you anyway to think you can go and achieve those big things?

    iii.   Write down your immediate gut response, along with any emotions that come up alongside that.

    iv.   Go through 4-5 major events in your life that have shaped where you are today. Write these out or play them out in your head.

    v.   Pay attention to your natural starting point—imagine a line where the 'raw events' are in the middle of the line, and underplaying is on the left and the fully embellished version on the right. Where on the spectrum would it lie?

    vi.   If you play with that and move it either to the left or to the right, what emotions come up for you?

3

WELL, WHO ARE YOU (REALLY)?

"Once we accept the fact that each of us embodies all the traits in the universe, we can stop pretending that we are not everything."—Debbie Ford, *The Dark Side of the Light Chasers*

❖ **Identity shifts**

You are bigger than you feel right now. Really.

I am telling you this because I have been exactly in your shoes and felt I would fight every step of the way to recognise and own my own value. Not because it wasn't there or others did not recognise it, but because I didn't recognise it myself.

The immediate weeks and months after I gave birth prematurely were some of my darkest and most vulnerable moments. I felt inadequate as a mother. A boss. A partner. A business owner. I considered throwing in the towel and walking away from my own business to start again from scratch. All while processing the shock and numbness of becoming a mother two months earlier than I had planned.

Until I realised that I was the one that needed to first BELIEVE in myself, in the power of my own vision, and OWN my intrinsic sense of value and worth, before anyone else could. I invested in deep coaching support.

This allowed me emotional space to process everything that had come along with the massive identity shift that had taken place. Certainly in becoming a mum now responsible for raising a tiny human, but also all the build-up that had happened in the years leading up to that.

The big, bold statements I used to make back in my corporate days, and even the long-term vision in the years when I first started my business, were in fact empty. A banner that I could carry to cover up the absence of truly believing in my own potential for greatness.

And this is something that we see time and time again in the clients that we coach.

Secretly, all we ever want is for someone to tell us that they see something greater in us than we are able to see for ourselves. And not just empty words of validation, but for someone to say it and truly mean it.

But the truth is that the most important person that sentence needs to come from is *you*.

❖ Louise: "Well, who am I?"

Louise was a brilliant and highly experienced senior marketing leader and brand strategist with a stellar career of over 20 years under her belt. She had won multiple awards as a creative and marketing director.

She had made the decision to go solo after experiencing the frustrations of a boxed-in corporate life, and knowing that she had a lot more to offer.

It was one of our early sessions. We were pulling together her One-Page Vision (the starting point of all work we do), where she experienced the familiar challenge of developing her big vision statement.

Version 1 was written almost like a box framed around something that felt 'realistic'. It was almost (as she later described) like something you could see at the top of a resume—a sort of summary statement of a tangible, measurable, and specific mission outcome.

I probed her. "This feels very tactile and specific. What is behind it? Why is this so important to you? How can it be stretched?"

Her reply: "There's a part of me that wonders—well, who am I to claim something so big, or to say I can do xyz?"

Exactly, who are you? There is so much to you. We forget that others will only ever get to see and experience a small piece of who we are, in relation to what matters to them.

❖ **Releasing the elephant – your corporate identity past**

There is a story of the four blind men and the elephant. The first blind man touched the elephant's trunk and said, "Oh my god, an elephant is like a large snake." The second blind man touched its leg and said, "Wow, it's actually like the trunk of a giant tree." The third blind man touched the side of the elephant and said, "No, no, you've got it all wrong—it's smooth and flat, like a big wall." Finally, the fourth blind man touched its tusk and said, "You guys must be crazy; it's long, pointy, hard, and sharp, like the weapon of a warrior."

All of those perspectives were true. All of those frames were true.

They just weren't complete.

No wonder when we leave that corporate world and go out on our own, we cannot see the truth of everything that we can be. We have only ever been defined by the blind (metaphorically speaking)—those who could see but a piece of us and not the whole.

You emanate energy from the moment you are born into this world. You are meant for impact.

Lost impact is the energy that is wasted as it dissipates because you have confined yourself to the frame of the blind. Such is the power of stepping forward to reveal your full vision and the potential and statement behind it.

❖ Awaken your true extraordinariness (your inner diamond)

Your true extraordinariness is the thing that makes you special and uniquely valuable to the world.

It is rarely something that you will wake up and realise yourself one day on your own. Quite often it is something we take for granted. It is so obvious and natural to us to use our gift that we never even think to value it.

It's mixed in with everything else that feels 'obvious' to us and is common sense—like turning off the tap when we are finished with it so as not to waste water… but again, that is not always common sense to everyone.

It is what we refer to in the work we do as your 'inner diamond'.

Who we are innately and how we think is created through our entire lifetime's worth of experiences, your unique personality, and even unconscious memories and experiences imprinted in your cell biology and passed down through generations.

Reconnecting with who you are firstly requires deep inward reflection. See the common threads of how you have impacted the circles of influence in your life, past and present. Friendships, close connections, family, workplaces, social and business circles.

What are the repeated themes that people you've encountered have said about you? Good and bad?

What happened in the generations before? Your parents and theirs? What life did they live, what were their primary relationships and the beliefs they held (or hold)?

What versions of truths are in the narratives they tell, and how has this imprinted on the stories and narratives you tell yourself today?

Awareness and that opening internally by you is the first step. To start to allow the light in to see that true extraordinariness within. It helps you to unravel all the mixing stories. Those that may not be yours, but that have been imprinted, that you've taken on as your own.

It helps you to let that go and start to really see yourself as who you truly are.

❖ Practical Section: Unlock your inner diamond (hidden truths in the path to self-actualisation)

Our stories begin well before we are even born and accelerate in our early years without us even being active in that process.

Neurobioligical studies on the Montessori philosophy show that the human child's brain absorbs information non-judgmentally between the ages of 0 and 3. It is simply taking everything in, making sense of the world, and adapting itself to the world around them.

This is the first phase where the 'truths' of the world and about yourself are first embedded into your brain—in other words, what we have been conditioned to believe or what we take for granted. Becoming aware of that is our first step in letting loose that which doesn't serve us, and empowering that which does.

The same lack of awareness occurs with our unique gifts and true extraordinariness. And this is the real reason we struggle to see our own inner diamond. It isn't until we come across someone who needs our help, and when they express the genuine appreciation that comes forth from that help, that we may get a hint that what we did wasn't 'just ordinary' at all.

And even so, it sometimes takes several repetitions of that happening—it takes you really recognising what that is, then doubling down on it. Then your inner diamond starts being really polished to shine and attract more of those whom you can help.

What often happens is that our filtering system, the system by which we take this gift for granted, is so strong that we often even filter out or push away acknowledgements or appreciation. This happens whenever we dismiss a thank you, a compliment. We say something like "It was nothing" or "It wasn't me, it was all you" rather than simply "Thank you" or "You're welcome."

We might think that we are just being humble in the moment. But really what we are doing is pushing away the signals that the universe is sending to us to put out more of that energy. The special sort that only you can give. By minimising its significance—by minimising our own significance—we ignore those signals and lose out on an opportunity to pursue self-actualisation.

Exercise: Uncover your inner diamond

So let's start to unpack and piece together your own 'elephant', as in the story of the blind men and the elephant.

Start by creating a picture of all the positive things people have ever told you, as well as what you innately know deep inside you.

What are the repeated patterns? Themes? Common threads?

If I asked you, "What is YOUR true extraordinariness?"—can you formulate a picture of what is at the heart of all that (your inner diamond)?

Because I promise you, it is there.

No matter what you currently believe or feel is possible for you.

And if you are reading this book, you are already on the path to awaken it.

And that is the exact purpose behind my writing this book.

4

FINDING YOUR REAL VALUE AND IMPACT IN THE WORLD

Your real impact is layers beneath the veneer and shiny, bold statements you make for others' benefit. Your real big hairy audacious goals and mission will only be revealed once you let that (the ego) go. Discover your real WHY.

❖ What exactly is impact?

It is my belief that true impact lies deep within that core, and it is through the peeling away, layer by layer, of the hard skins we have built to reach and reconnect with that core of who we are—strengthening that, refocusing that, sprinkling it with a dose of "I believe in you"—that that impact starts to come alive.

No longer anchored to external validation and trophies, but radiating from the very being of within with a desire to help and improve.

Impact, in my view, is therefore defined simply as your inner capacity to improve and to better someone else's life — and in this way make the world a better place.

That impact encompasses all the pieces that you give. All the pieces that you live and breathe. The parts you show, and the parts you don't. It's the darkness that helps you connect with someone buried in struggle. It's the light that shows them the hopes, excitement, and dreams that lie ahead.

Uncovering your true impact is a process of confronting both your 'light' and 'dark' sides– formative mentors, experiences and tough challenges (especially in early life and career phases). Below I share a few stories of how my own impact came to be.

❖ Mentorship and early lessons – the 'spark' of belief

It was my first day meeting her. My new boss—Daphne. I was a junior specialist in a biotech firm, in my early twenties. I had spent the three days prior sick as a dog in bed with a bad stomach flu—a rarity, as I didn't often get sick, and I was kicking myself with the timing.

I remember hoping that it didn't impact her first impression of me, that she wouldn't think I was someone who would be taking sick days all the time.

I was young, ambitious, and really wanted to get ahead in my career.

She had a little notebook that was already halfway filled with all the notes from her different meetings with multiple levels of the leadership and getting to know the team. She asked me to go through all the projects and activities I had been involved with to date. Then she asked me about my ambitions.

How did I want to develop, and how did I want to grow?

I was cautious. Previously, answering this question had backfired on me and I was seen as uncommitted to my role and position, creating strained relationships with my managers. To my surprise, she was extremely supportive, and even promised to speak to the leadership team to see how they could be more involved in helping me pave a path towards career progression.

Daphne was the first mentor that believed in me before I believed in myself, and I still attribute much of my later career developments to when that spark was first ignited.

Your formative adult path is often shaped in your early twenties, just as there is very much a formative period in childhood. And we underestimate the impact that encouragement, support, and space to expand and grow can shape us during this period.

Our brains are actually still in development until we are 25 years old. As such, much of what happens during this period can in fact accelerate or hinder our own sense of self-belief.

Think back to your first mentor. Someone who was a mentoring presence in your life.

This usually isn't a formal role, but someone who was guiding you during a critical early phase in your career.

It may even have been a friend, a family member, or even sometimes yourself.

How did that shape your view on who you are and your outlook on the impact you believe it is possible for you to achieve today?

❖ **Childhood armour and corporate power plays– seeing beyond resilience to discover your deeper core value**

My younger years were spent mostly moving around. I was the new girl every year, moving from country to country and from school to school. I had a new best friend every year. And by the age of 12, I was entering my seventh consecutive school.

It was the feeling of being 'different' and 'wrong' from a young age. At home, things were equally challenging. My relationship with my mother was difficult growing up and often fraught with conflict.

These events never shook my sense of self and the potential I believed I held within me to create.

But it did also create a thick skin and outer armour that I then had to learn to break down once I entered the business world and began to rediscover my sense of authenticity.

Fast-forwarding to my corporate career, I found myself facing a new kind of battlefield– one of power plays and toxic behaviours that demanded a different type of armour.

A top-level portfolio executive angrily stormed into the room, irritated with an group email reply I had sent in response to his that dared to suggest an alternative way of handling a client I was directly responsible for.

"I'll have you know that I don't need telling about how to handle clients."

Gotta love that highly charged and ego-driven environment of corporate management consultancies. He followed that confrontation with a pointed email copying several of my superiors, dismissing and breaking down my suggestion as inexperienced nonsense.

Then there was my client as a young first-time account director in my early twenties. A challenging man. He would show up to our meetings completely disengaged (unless he had already cancelled last minute with a simple decline, with no note of explanation—which was also usual practice for him). He would sit in the meetings staring at his laptop the entire time while grunting acknowledgements at what I was saying. Once he literally told me to get out of his office while pointing at the door.

This all happened during my first year in the company. Alongside a whirlwind of events.

Massive power play. And highly toxic behaviour.

It shocks me even writing down these stories that this kind of behaviour happened, and even more so that I took these events without batting an eye.

Looking back now, with more maturity, I recognise that those situations called for something different—not just resilience, but the courage to call out bullying and toxic behaviour for what it was. At the time, though, it honestly didn't even penetrate.

My resilience evolved into emotional distance, allowing me to survive but without confronting deeper issues at play.

It was all these events and factors however that created the push to discover and the drive to continue to believe in my own potential. It is what created a sort of unique ability in me to see past the negative stories, protective fronts, and deflective behaviours that people put up to the world, to see deeply into their hidden psyche and potential for impact within. What I would describe as one of my 'core values'.

The essence of the section is about self-discovery beyond resilience–which has often become a defence mechanism or survival strategies.

To really discover your *core value*– the qualities and beliefs that define you at your most genuine, the inner foundation that drives your actions, passions, and interactions once you shed the defences shaped by past experiences.

I wonder if you recognise this in your own experiences? What shaped you, and your 'core value' as a person? What armours did you create as you entered into, and throughout, your career? What did you then need to shed in order to fully embrace your authentic self?

❖ **Practical Section: Exploring your dark side and recognising your core value**

Every person has a capacity for making an impact. They have a gift that is unique to them, and that gift has its dark and light side. It is in the exploration of the dark side that we discover its depths and can channel that in healthy ways that do not become overcompensation.

We develop a thick skin over time to shield and protect our dark sides, the painful memories that make us feel like we are not enough—so much so, adding on layer after layer (achievements, status objects, titles), that we forget what is truly beneath all of that.

Impact becomes surface level, and we feel disconnected from the outcomes as a result.

Exercise: Train your brain to start recognising your core value

To rewire and retrain yourself to start recognising your core value, keep a journal of positive statements that people have said about you to go back and read whenever you start to feel the seeds of doubt. Take yourself back to the ones that most touched you—they are the ones that point to where your true extraordinariness lies. They are the ones you feel deep in your gut, a sense of resonance with the seed of your inner truth.

They are also the ones about which doubt will creep in, making you question whether they matter or convincing you to automatically dismiss them as insignificant.

PART TWO

HOLDING SPACE AND RECONNECTING

"The active mind is difficult to tame, flighty and wandering where it will: taming it is essential, leading to the joy of wellbeing."—Buddha

5

BLOCK #1: YOUR INNER EGO & CRITIC

"There are enough barriers in the world without ourselves being one of them."

—*Jacinda Ardern*

❖ The voice

You know it.

It's the voice that shows up when you are about to share that post, film a video, write a new blog, record or be interviewed on a podcast. And you hear it say, "That's so surface level and generic, what makes you think you are sharing something of value?"

When you are about to raise your prices. And you hear, "But what if they walk away because they don't think it's worth it?"

When you feel that push within to step into something new and unknown. And it says, "But what if you fail and fall on your face?"

"What if everything you have worked SO HARD to build—reputation, respect, income—all falls apart and you lose it all?"

I have this inner voice right now running in parallel even as I am writing these words. My biggest lesson during my own long journey of self-growth has been realising that the inner critic voice is not an enemy, but a protector of our deepest inner child.

The one with big dreams, limitless self-expression, and unbound creativity.

The inner child that needs encouragement. A warm, soothing hug. The feeling of safety in moments of discomfort. In knowing they can jump, and that you—the adult you—are going to support them through whatever happens on the other side. And that you already have the inner strength to go through with it.

Because the reward on the other side is ever so sweet and so, so worth it.

❖ **Your inner critic is not your enemy**

In my first year of business, I attended the business lifestyle retreat that I mentioned previously—the one that promised to 'kill and destroy' my inner critic in the space of 12 days.

And kill and destroy my inner critic, it did. At least for quite a runway following that retreat.

It was also a period where I made some rather brash and, looking back, not exactly the smartest decisions when it came to my business. Including hiring a full-time team—before I was mentally ready, and before the business was financially steady.

These are the dangers of overriding 'critical thinking', which we need, and jumping straight into 'doing'. Before **grounded** self-clarity and direction.

While I don't regret the decisions and path I took, and hiring the team meant I got the chance to work with some brilliant young talent up close, it challenged me to learn and be confronted with the boundaries and gaps of my own leadership capacity at the time. In a tumultuous startup environment, no less.

Full healing and embracing of the inner critic and ego that holds you back does not require squashing, killing, or destroying it. It requires acceptance and love. It requires simply trusting in and holding space for it from within.

Because without that supportive foundation, nurture, and follow-up after, it becomes another vulnerability, wrapped up in another layer of protection. Like a wound that's been ripped open, only to be replaced by another scab that never fully heals what's beneath.

Your inner critic is not your enemy.

I often coach my high-achieving clients with strong inner critic voices to imagine their inner critic as a caring family member or friend who wants to look out for them.

It is our automatic protection mechanism. And in this way, it is helpful to see it as an ally and not a threat.

So the next time the inner critic voice strikes up within you, the trick is to envision yourself saying to them, "Thank you, I SO appreciate your care. I don't know if I'm ready or not. But I'm going to do it anyway."

❖ **Mirror, mirror on the wall, who is the most critical of them all? (Meet 'you', your inner critic)**

Let me get vulnerable with you for a moment.

Some of my own most important moments of growth when it came to my inner critic came through the intimate space of my marriage.

The harshest judgments we impose on others are often the biggest ones that we have towards ourselves. Whether you're aware of it or not.

The early years of my relationship with my husband, Dimitri, were rocky ones. Ambitious and driven, I couldn't understand how someone, especially someone as intelligent and capable as he was, could be working on their dreams while simultaneously spending weekends and downtime relaxing and playing video games.

Was this laziness? Surely that was the time to be working on your dreams?!

It didn't become clear to me until much later that all that judgment and do-do-do energy I was holding and pushing was only suffocating the space for our relationship to breathe. Suffocating my own energy to pursue my dreams. But also suffocating the open space for my husband to be able to flourish in his own time and at his own pace.

This has also been one of my biggest life lessons of growth—to learn the importance of rest and relaxation. And I do believe my husband has come into my life exactly for that reason. Dimitri and I are very different people, and that is a good thing—we create balance in each other. And for the record, my husband is actually a very accomplished person in his own field.

As we navigated our marriage, learning each other's mindsets and accepting each other and ourselves for who we are, it made me reflect on what it was that I was judging myself on.

What was the criticism and doubt I was holding towards myself? And was I projecting it?

Perhaps the big part of me was in do-do-do mode in an attempt to feel like things were moving forward and in control, but the truth was that I was spinning my wheels, and exhausted, then resenting the fact that I saw someone doing what I actually truly needed, which was rest and the permission to slow down.

In other words, it was about the illusion of control, rather than actually being in control.

The next time you catch yourself criticising someone, or receive a judgment from someone on you, it is a space created that invites you to assess:

What internal criticism (or judgment) do you—or they—have on yourself, or they on themselves, that is being reflected back?

What quality, characteristic, or behaviour—past or present—is it that you are silently judging yourself on (in other words, that you haven't fully accepted about yourself)?

By judging the other, you are rejecting that quality and denying its existence—invalidating its origins within you. It is a rejection of a part of you.

❖ **The 4 keys to overcoming block #1 (your inner ego & critic)**

There are 4 important aspects to overcome this first block of your inner critic and ego:

1. Compassion - Being kind to yourself

2. Acceptance - Recognising and acknowledging your inner voice and boundaries

3. Honour - Learning to saying no

4. Let go - Of fear of losing relationships

Not doing these things repeatedly will always come with the cost of compromising our true selves, and a build-up of tension that will eventually erupt.

Sometimes we just don't know where our fuse is, or when it will unexpectedly get lit.

It was Australia Day. I was home for a big family reunion—the first after four years thanks to Covid. We decided to make it a beach day and drive out to a faraway (and hopefully less busy) beach down the south coast.

As with all big family reunions after a long period, there was a definite build-up of emotion until then. We hadn't been able to physically be together for years. And the entire family hadn't gotten together like that for at least eight years, living in close quarters and over an extended period of two months.

My husband had not joined me on this trip, and I sorely missed the support for re-centring and perspective in the midst of the collective fluctuating family emotions.

Perhaps it was the feeling of being left out. Having a one-year-old toddler in tow definitely leaves you out for certain activities. Perhaps it was the stress of not feeling in control of time and headspace to get things done. The 11-hour time difference away from our core business. Perhaps it was the feeling of having had to hold the charged emotional energy of everyone else, including my one-year-old, for the entire trip.

Either way, on that day—I flipped.

My mum and I had been driving in circles searching for parking for close to 45 minutes, after already completing a one-hour drive. The flip was over a parking space that my sisters failed to hold for us.

One flipped switch sets off another flipped switch, and suddenly I was in a raging argument with my brother-in-law.

The day felt ruined. I sat silently on the beach rug with tears welling in my eyes. My one-year-old, Aria, was looking at me confused, and my sisters sat awkwardly as my brother-in-law and I fumed silently in our own aftermaths from the fight.

Eventually I made the move to make it right and apologise during a walk. It was a tough day. What that day taught me was the importance of being kind. Of holding space, especially for our own humanity and inner critic, with compassion.

It felt really hard not to beat myself up. It felt like all the hard work on personal growth I had done on myself had become undone. I practiced being kind. I practiced giving myself a mental warm hug.

Ironically, the one person that stuck up for me the most that day was Mum, and it was through a simple act.

Acceptance.

She had a quiet word with my brother-in-law as I walked onto the balcony for some air—"That is Angela, she's more direct."

And if there is only one thing you take from this chapter, let it be this: to practice acceptance. All the truths, all the ugliness, all the darkness— give it a hug.

Allowing space for our inner voices to exist and be heard, beyond our ego and inner critic, begins with learning to be kind to yourself. Only by doing so can you truly learn to be kind, less judgmental, and less critical towards others.

   ANGELA TSAI

❖ **Practical Section: Turning the ego and inner critic into your ally**

Your ego / inner critic actually has the potential to become your biggest ally if you allow it—as long as you know the space in which it plays and keep it in balance.

For me personally, it was the realisation that the ego / inner critic within me was also what had driven me to success. It simply isn't healthy to have zero ego at all. In fact, psychological theories even go as far as to emphasise the idea that balanced ego (rather than absence of ego) is essential for mental health.

Every experience and person in your life is there for a reason, to teach you something. And each trigger is there to activate a new realisation and growth in you.

It is up to you whether you will step into that.

Download your free worksheet here, which includes a section on tuning into your inner critic:
https://growyourbrandwithimpact.com/self-reflection-gybwi

Tune into your inner critic: Where are you holding back?

Write down 8-10 things that you KNOW you need to put into action and put in the right column immediate thoughts that come to your mind.

5% Conscious Mind

- I need to increase my prices

- I want to write a blog / become a thought leader

- ___________________________

- ___________________________

- ___________________________

- ___________________________

- ___________________________

- ___________________________

- ___________________________

95% Unconscious Mind

- What if I don't have enough clients?

- What if no one finds my opinion worthy?

- ___________________________

- ___________________________

- _______________________________
- _______________________________
- _______________________________
- _______________________________
- _______________________________

Exercise: Turn the ego and inner critic into your ally

Step 1 - The next time you want or need something but you feel an inner resistance—a voice of caution that stems from fear—tune into what it is saying (use the worksheet on the previous page as a guide).

Step 2 - Treat it as an over-caring family member or friend.

Step 3 - Listen to your gut instinct.

Step 4 - Reassure the inner critic that you will be fine and do it anyway.

6

BLOCK #2: FEAR & DOUBT

"The Ego said: 'I don't like this one. I don't like that one. This one hurt me. This one betrayed me. This one took from me and never gave back. But I don't want to hate them, as hatred starts to suffocate me after a while. What do I do?'

"The Soul replied: 'Then find a new way to love them. Love them from afar. Love them by wishing them well. Love them by understanding it is the weakness of their soul. Love them by understanding it is their pain and fear. Love them where they are. And love them by asking for God's love, strength and wisdom to reach their soul.'"—Richa Rana

❖ **Subconscious 'bubble wrap'**

Fear and doubt enter into our lives from day 1 of our time here on Earth. They are a natural part of who we are—as natural as their opposites, courage and confidence. It is something I was a front-seat witness to in my then-one-year-old as she moved through milestone after milestone. Babies thrive in environments when nothing is forced—even in the moments of fear and doubt—and they are encouraged to move beyond at their own pace.

So why shouldn't that be the same in every single stage of our life?

Fears and doubts, when you really boil it down, only ever come from three sources:

1. Learned experiences through our interactions with the world, from childhood all the way to adulthood and now

2. Generational pass-downs (genetic memories imprinted in our cellular biology)

3. Collective pass-throughs (as herd animals at the core, our survival relies on collective intelligence, and we are always influenced by those around us to learn from their experiences)

And every single fear comes back to the fear of death. The fear of rejection. The latter, in our biology as herd mammals, ultimately leads to death. The antidote to fear and doubt is the feeling of safety. At least the CREATION of that feeling.

What we often do not realise is the degree of artificial safety we've created around ourselves to avoid even the feeling or recognising the rise of fear and doubt. I call this unconscious bubble-wrapping.

In my case, and without realising it, it was a mechanism I had lived with almost my entire life. For the first 34 years of my life, this was the state I had created for myself. Moving into corporate, relying on the security of an ambitiously driven career and a solid paycheque each month. The employer felt safe. Things were on my terms. Or so it felt. And I never left a job without another one already lined up.

When the biotech company I was working for started showing signs of financial instability, and was in the early stages of being bought out by a large pharma—I got myself out of there before the smell of redundancy even hit the air.

Like a video game character, I leapt to the next level and onto the next cloud before the cloud beneath my feet had the chance to dissipate.

Fears and doubts have their purpose in keeping us safe. But listening only to this voice is also the singular path that blocks us from growth. Bubble-wrapping isn't the solution if what our heart truly desires is to go after our dream.

Bravery and confidence are not the same thing. But bravery, or courage, is what is going to help you build confidence and belief in yourself over time. Continuing to hold ourselves in a bubble-wrapped state, over time, creates numbing, frustrating resentment, bitterness, and a sense of resignation.

And that's your choice. It is the price of a continued feeling of 'safety'.

So, what is more important to you? There is no right or wrong answer here.

❖ Re-establishing our relationship with fear and doubt

What would life be like if you had no fear or doubt? What would you do? And how rewarding would it be if you didn't have that fear or doubt?

I believe as children it is so important to establish that relationship with fear and doubt, to know that it is normal and a sign of growth.

And sometimes, we need to establish that relationship again in our adult lives. Especially when we transition into new phases—moving from a structured corporate career to running your own business is a perfect example of this, when we start to feel uncertain on our feet and like children again.

How do you overcome fear and doubt from stopping yourself from progressing?

Stop asking for permission.

I'm not saying to do things alone, and not have people help, cheerlead, and encourage you on the way. But be selective about the coach, mentor, supporter, or guide that you bring in.

For the 'sensitive projects'—especially those you still feel fragile about and you are building confidence in--surround yourself only with those that will encourage and nurture your innate ability to keep going. Those that empower you to trust yourself, rather than telling you what to do, while gently suggesting alternative ways forward.

Not the ones that will challenge and overwhelm through critical feedback too early, which may only overwhelm ideas in the sensitive, fragile early stages and in turn manifesting more fears and doubts that will paralyse you and prevent you from taking action. There is a time and place for critique and feedback, and it's your call to allow it in only when you are ready.

Confidence comes through action.

The early stages are about building your internal compass to trust yourself, rather than creating the disbalance of dependency on others' opinions. It is about learning to shut out all the voices outside of you, and learning to trust yourself and listen to your gut.

❖ Practical Section: 'Overcoming' imposter syndrome

Imposter syndrome is never the problem—a lack of it is.

In the words of motivational speaker Mel Robbins, "Imposter syndrome is not actually a problem. It is simply a sign of a shift. A sign you are doing something you haven't done enough before." It is, in fact, a sign that you are leaning into bravery and courage.

When my business partner, Cristina, finally decided to let go of her secure corporate job after being one foot in for a year and a half, and join me full-time in the business, it was all meant to be a steady ramp-up: two and a half full months of handover and stabilising on the revenue side of things before I was due to give birth to my daughter.

Unfortunately, life had other plans, and my daughter came premature—exactly two months early. Meaning Cristina was thrust into chaos while in the midst of handing over her own job. She could have easily said at that moment that the instability was too much and chosen other plans to secure her income. But instead, she leaned right in.

Fully lean into that bravery and courage, which means doing the things that you still feel uncomfortable about. Close your eyes and take that little leap of faith, over and over.

Make that post where you are showing yourself. Reach out to those people you need to. Make that pitch on the sales call. Put that offer in front of someone, even if it is not fully ready. Dare to allow yourself, to invite someone to say yes or no.

This is what will build your confidence over time.

When you are never feeling imposter syndrome, it is a sign that you are likely keeping yourself in that bubble-wrapped artificial safety, rather than chasing the full potential for growth inside of you.

Exercise: What are the sources of your fears?

Understanding and shining light on your fear allows you to objectively see the source and choose how you want to deal with it.

Start noting down your fears, and start to separate these into the three buckets we discussed previously in this section. When you do feel a rise of fear at any moment, write it down.

1. Learned experiences through our interactions with the world, from childhood all the way to adulthood and now

2. Generational pass-downs (genetic memories imprinted in our cellular biology)

3. Collective pass-throughs (as herd animals at our core, our survival relies on collective intelligence, and we are always influenced by those around us to learn from their experiences)

Which of these three categories do you feel is the source?

Can you nail it down to a specific event? Do you listen to it (the specific fear)?

Is it valid? Is it yours? Is it true?

The goal of this exercise is to start to train you to recognise the real feelings of fear and doubt, because in fact, our brains have become so accustomed to training us away from even realising and feeling that this is happening.

What is really interesting, though, is when we start to recognise our automatic antidotes to this feeling of fear and doubt.

7

BLOCK #3: DISCONNECTION WITH YOUR EMOTIONAL SELF

"People have two basic needs. Attachment and authenticity. When authenticity threatens attachment… attachment trumps authenticity."—Dr Gabor Mate

❖ How we lose connection with our emotional self

When I moved into the hectic world of consulting, I thought I'd made it. I was working for one of the most prestigious global consulting firms in the world, and it was my absolute dream. I didn't care that people didn't talk to each other at the coffee machine, or in the elevator.

While there were many positives—brilliant mentors I met, and growth I'm thankful for to this day—I do believe this was the place I lost my connection with my soul.

In those first two years, I averaged about five hours' sleep a night, and I spent three and a half to four hours in the car each day. I was involved in a car accident twice within the same month due to lack of focus while driving home. Between the crazy hours working, then finishing off my master's thesis during late nights and weekends, I became completely disconnected from living. And my relationship at that time completely broke down.

While my career was progressing, I was a nervous wreck, a ball of stress— lashing out if anyone demanded my time outside of work and my master's, forgoing food and sleep, and developing physical twitches when my phone would buzz as emails came in—bang, bang, bang, every few minutes.

For my entire career as far back as I can remember, I fiercely separated the buckets of work and personal life. Nobody from my personal life needed to be part of my work life, and my work life was strictly kept there.

This is the biggest lesson we can possibly realise: that there never was or needed to be any separation.

When we switch off parts of ourselves in order to be accepted, we sacrifice authentic self-expression and connection with our soul.

In your career, how much have you dared to fully be yourself? How often have you said yes when your heart, soul, and body were saying no? How much of that have you sacrificed in order to maintain attachment within a specific environment or group and be accepted by your colleagues, peers, team, friends, superiors?

Is it any wonder, then, that in entering your own business, you still carry that? "Will I be fully accepted if people see the true me, and not the version I've projected all these years until now?"

These old versions are the ones that held the status, respect, titles. All the pieces of armour that unknowingly keep us trapped in the cycle of continued disconnection from our emotions. From ourselves.

❖ How this prevents you from moving forward

About 60% of communication and persuasion comes through *pathos* (emotion). Around 30% is *logos* (logic) and 10% is *ethos* (credibility).

I first learned about the concept of pathos, ethos, and logos in a leadership training I was part of several years ago. Pathos is the key to attention-grabbing headlines. Journalism's big secret—the 'lede'—getting right to the heart of why people should care and the emotions.

Personally, I have always struggled with connecting to that and bringing it out. This is usually the first sign of self-filtering, not letting it out. A byproduct of suppressing connection with our emotions through numbing and forcing our entire lives.

Yet, if 60% of our ability to communicate, connect, and convince comes through emotion (pathos), and we have largely learnt to suppress it, it's easy to see why our ability to move forward towards our goals is limited.

The trouble is that as we learn to numb ourselves to negative versions of ourselves and our emotions, we numb ourselves to all emotions, and struggle then to reconnect with them later on. It blocks our ability to respond and express ourselves spontaneously and naturally. We come across as forced and awkward because of the conflict happening within us.

Emotions are happening, but our body and mind are unable to channel them.

"Just be yourself" is probably one of the most useless pieces of advice in this sense when the trouble is that most of us have completely forgotten who we even are.

Within institutions like corporations, where it is just about playing in the bounds, you never actually need those emotions.

 In fact, conformity is encouraged. "He or she is a good cultural fit." It's what maintains your ability to remain 'attached', never a threat to the environment you are in. But at what cost?

The real movers and shakers in the world, though, have the strong pull within them to express themselves fully, authentically.

If you are reading this, you are that. You have the inner desire within to express yourself. Even if it means going against the grain and at the risk of losing attachment to the communities you have known and felt safe within up until now.

But these people are also the ones that will actuate real change within exactly those communities, creating the shifts and changes in thinking that will envelop the progression towards something.

New CEOs that take over companies are either maintainers or disruptors. In the real balance of the world, there is a need for both. Constant disruption is exhausting and unsustainable. But maintain the same pace for too long, and stagnation will lead to eventual atrophy.

The same applies to your own pursuit of your dream.

❖ How to unlock and reconnect with your true self

The first step to reconnect with anything is being able to name and recognise it. In order to reconnect you have to first see something and realise it is there. There is no shutting it down.

People often underplay the trauma and disconnection they may have experienced.

The external circumstances come in varying degrees… but at the root of it all, it comes back to your earliest moments of attachment and ability to safely express yourself authentically and remain accepted. Rediscover and unlocking often begins with the sharing of how you are really feeling with someone you trust, and finding that space of acceptance, even as you share who you truly are.

Our own journeys to rediscover connection come from the unexpected moments of sharing.

Mine was this. I was standing under an umbrella in Amsterdam, waiting out the rain. I was with my younger sister, who was visiting from her exchange trip in Sweden—sharing that my relationship was failing. A scene that should be so normal between sisters, but isn't.

I hadn't really spent time with my sister for about nine years since I left home, went to uni, then moved to the Netherlands.

I still remember my sisters as the little girls that I left behind—11 and

8 years old, respectively, when I left home. It was the first time we had spent quality time together and were getting to know each other as adults. I was always the 'cool sister' living abroad in Europe; I wanted to be the role model, strong, with the perfect career and life.

The reality behind the scenes was that with my crazy work and study schedule, and complete emotional and physical exhaustion, my relationship was falling apart and I didn't have the emotional equipment to deal with it. It was under that umbrella, before my sister was about to meet some friends at an Amsterdam coffee shop, while we waited for the rain to stop in front of the Bijenkorf, that I burst into tears and shared the real struggle I was having.

Healing your past from a place of opening up (in a trusted space) and self-compassion is so important to reconnect with that emotional self.

If as children, we never learnt to properly process emotions because we never learnt to identify them—this will carry into adulthood.

And it often occurs because we have learnt as a child that our negative emotions are disturbing or inconvenient to others. Our expressions of self are not wanted and are therefore shut down.

It becomes our default reaction. Yet learning to hold space for those emotions and process them is the key to growth, and to developing healthy coping mechanisms that don't involve disconnecting from ourselves.

The way I have discovered to do this, is to **talk to yourself, as if you are your child.**

The journey to regain connection to your emotional self (and full self-expression) begins as simply as learning to be comfortable with having emotions.

Think of a recent event that triggered you or gives you an uncomfortable feeling or memory—sit in that. Can you identify the emotion you are feeling about it?

Talk to yourself as if you are your child. Can you empathise with the 'you' that is having that feeling?

Let's say that you had an important presentation or conversation—perhaps a sales call with an important potential client, or regarding a promotion—and you felt like you botched it up. You walked away angry at yourself that you didn't handle it as well as you could, and you screwed up your chances.

Can you be compassionate towards that version of you?

Are the words you are normally saying to yourself those of self-criticism or defeat? Perhaps along the lines of "So stupid of me" or "I wish I could have been more assertive in dealing with that"?

Or a defeated "Oh well" while secretly beating yourself up inside?

Sensitive yet ambitious high achievers have a default tendency to beat themselves up. While they will be angry at the other person, and frustrated at the situation, at the deepest level, the anger and frustration is towards themselves.

What if you were to flip that towards acceptance, compassion, and space—focusing less on the judgment of the outcome, but on the acceptance and encouragement towards effort, recognising that you did your very best in that moment?

Replace those words with acknowledging the emotion and feeling it, fully.

Disappointment, anger, sadness. Describe it, and tie it to the real cause.

"You're angry that it didn't work out. You worked so hard and were hoping this would go well."

Let yourself be with those feelings, and don't force yourself to think positively just yet.

There will come the time for positivity and reframing that once you've allowed the space for it.

It is a fact that not every single go will be a score, not every push will succeed. We often give up sooner because we miss seeing the bigger picture of the success on the other side.

We let our emotions and the fear and doubt get the better of us, rather than channelling it and seeing it as yet another step.

Exercise: 4 steps to reconnect with yourself emotionally

1. Fully express the trigger and emotion. I recommend keeping a trigger journal somewhere with easy access—I use the DayOne app on my phone. Write down everything and try to

describe how you feel, including the behaviour or event that triggered it. Use the emotion wheel as a tool to identify words.

2. Acknowledge and validate that emotion.

3. Let yourself be with those feelings, and don't force yourself to think positively. Let it process and flow through you.

4. Once that has processed, take some time to gain perspective.

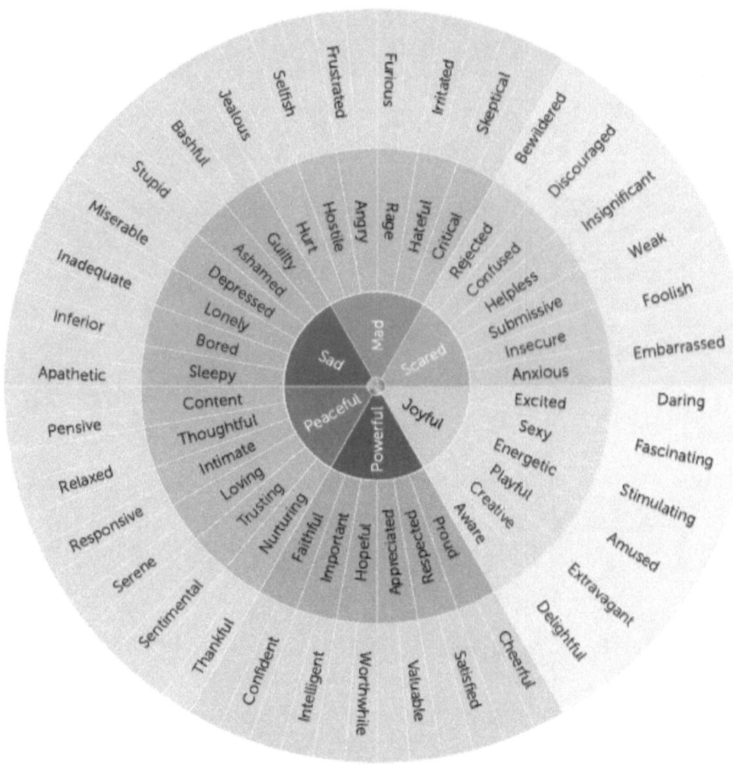

Source: The Feeling Wheel, Dr Gloria Willcox, 1982

8

BLOCK #4: LETTING GO OF THE GRIND

'I often ask myself what the purpose of life is. I conclude that it is to be happy. [...] Today, the world is mostly focussed on external development. However, ancient Indian traditions emphasise looking within to find the real source of joy.'

—*The Dalai Lama*

❖ Identifying your version of 'the grind'

There are four main types of 'grind' that you may recognise, in yourself or others. You may even think about other ways that it shows up.

Reactive grind: Jumping straight into reactive action, pedalling like crazy.

This can show up in the form of diving into your emails, admin, or operations. Or spending hours on social media, keeping your head buried in client delivery work. Or spending hours tinkering with your website.

Underlying cause—a compulsion to feel busy and productive, often as a response to stress or uncertainty.

Guilt-driven grind: Punishing yourself by forcing yourself to work and forgo relaxation or pleasure when you feel like something has gone wrong, instead forcing yourself to fix it before you can relax.

The underlying thought is "I've wasted my time, so in turn I need to suffer and be unhappy" (but also thereby producing bad work).

Projected grind: Frustration and blaming external situations that meant you haven't been able to get things done.

Underlying cause—stress or inability to manage workload or prioritise effectively, resulting in interpersonal conflict or distraction.

Unfocused grind: The discomfort of not having focus or knowing what you need to do, and therefore jumping straight into 'doing'— similar to the first type, which is usually anchored towards others' goals… jumping into operational activity or helping others.

Underlying cause—discomfort with ambiguity and leaping into action to mitigate feelings of ineffectiveness or aimlessness.

Whichever version of grind you experience, what is clear is that you are not in control in that moment, despite feeling like you are—and you are not operating with the clear headspace to move towards your higher-level goals.

❖ The price of 'the grind' is always loss of connection

One of my earliest memories is watching this grind in action.

My dad graduated engineering in the top percentile within the top three universities in Taiwan. He had his pick of jobs and was definitely an eligible bachelor. My dad never really needed to grind; he had his future cut out for him. But it was the normal thing to do in Asian culture: you work hard and provide for your family.

My mum insisted on moving us to Australia. It wasn't the most straightforward path, and it certainly made life much more challenging than the very comfortable life we would have been able to live in Taiwan.

It meant my dad went from top graduate and top desirable candidate that would have his pick of companies and jobs, to starting from the bottom. Battling language barriers to even be considered for a starting position in a mediocre firm.

He wasn't successful. And after finishing his MBA (which was the route he took to be able to move his family to Australia), he had to return to Taiwan so that he could continue working and provide for his family living overseas.

Our dreams and motivations are often shaped through dysfunctions and hardships we experience through life.

My dad grew up in a family profoundly marked by fractures in core relationships. An unfaithful father, eight siblings living in resentment towards their father, and his mother passing away during his teenage years. His only and biggest hope and dream was to create his own 'perfect family'.

He took me with him back to Taiwan for a year when I was 9 years old, where for a while I lived with my grandparents.

I still remember him taking me to his offices on the weekend when he had to finish some piece of work… and I got to see his living quarters. It was a small dormitory. Barren and simple with a single bed. Around 12 square meters in total, with a desk in the corner and a window.

Outside was a communal kitchen and a communal bathroom. I remember seeing the state of the shower and bath and scrunching my face because it looked unclean—I guess that's what happens when you have 12 men living single lives and sharing a dormitory space.

Soon after we moved to Taiwan, my dad found us a flat and we moved in together. But life was definitely a grind even then.

I was envious of my friend at school; I would join her after school when she went for her piano lessons. Dad couldn't afford to send me, as all his money was being sent overseas… but he would put my hands on his while we were riding on his scooter and encourage me to pretend to play.

It still shocks me to know just how successful a career path my dad actually had, and that he had all the potential to reach the top—all his peers that graduated with him at the same level became CEOs or heads of big companies.

Because we always lived, for as long as I can remember, as if we had no money.

It was the price he paid to be able to eventually retire early at the age of 45 and move back to Australia to reunite with his family with a healthy retirement fund and savings—after a seven-year absence—without the pressure of needing to start grinding again.

Sadly, the family disintegrated almost immediately upon the reunification and my parents separated.

The price of 'the grind' is, almost always, the loss of connection.

Often the grind and working for it is all about helping us to get to this perceived state of stability. Utopia.

But is it at the cost of losing sight of the experience and journey, and what's really important, the 'something more', and our connections with ourselves and relationships that made all this matter in the first place?

I am so grateful to my dad for the sacrifices he made. But it is also a valuable life lesson I received from him. One that he recounted in his personal memoir that he shared with my sisters and I: to honour the here and now.

This is why my business partner, Cristina, and I decided to pivot our business to a 16-hour work week model so as not to lose precious connection time with our daughters in those critical early years.

So much of our own lessons in terms of our relationship with 'the grind' and working hard come from cultural and family expectations passed down, purposely or simply generationally.

I wonder if you are aware of your own roots when it comes to your own relationship with the grind?

Do you recognise any of the types of grind I mentioned above? And where the roots of this behaviour come from?

Reflection: A lesson in play

My husband is probably one of the most intelligent people that I have ever met. Yet our pathways and philosophies to learning could not have been more different growing up.

I was on the pathway of discipline and traditional learning, with every single day filled with school, homework, and after-school curricular activities without a lot of play.

And while my husband's mum drilled into him the importance of academic achievement, there was plenty of time spent on play. He still claims that most of the knowledge he gained growing up was through playing video games!

For me, the grind and constantly having a filled schedule followed me throughout my career into a hectic decade in the world of management consulting and straight into my entrepreneurial business life.

Storytelling and play are inherent parts of our humanness that we have forgotten and mostly lost in our busy lives. Yet with play, my husband may have been onto something.

Play is also the basis of myths and stories, and memories that actually stick and remain when it comes to humankind and our ancestors' lives.

What if the constant push for productivity is the very thing holding you back? Imagine for a moment, what might open up if you allowed play to take over, just for a while. What 'spaces' in your life, business and work, could you make room for, to allow for this play?

❖ Have you lost perspective with the grind?

Letting go of the grind is easier than we think—however, it takes courage to be silent. To be still.

Christmas 2021. It was the final few months before the baby arrived. Or so I thought.

I was working day and night, every single weekend, to get a working 'campaign funnel' and baby-proof the business… with a steady flow of leads. Losing sleep despite being heavily pregnant. 2021 was a burnout year. In cash. In the team. In me.

These patterns are often so ingrained in us that nothing shakes them until there is a big and sudden interruption.

For me, this was the early arrival of my daughter just two weeks after that crazy Christmas.

It took the literal taking away of space to 'grind' and the shock of needing to settle into this new identity as a mother with a newborn (and a premature one at that), spending 8-10 hours each day at the hospital for the first month, to start deconditioning from that auto-response tendency to jump into the grind.

In the moments of stress, it is easiest for us to fall back onto operational and delivery work.

This was what Cristina, my business partner, experienced when she first took over for me, having just freshly quit her corporate job, during those first intensive weeks post-birth.

It feels busy, it feels good, it feels like you're making progress.

The grind is our safety net—we don't realise that it keeps us locked in. We keep going because it gives us a feeling that we are moving forward, that we are in control. But actually, we are often simply occupying ourselves with busywork and losing sight of the bigger picture—not realising we are running in circles.

It takes courage to step out of the grind. The act of stopping forces us to confront the real issue that we need to deal with, to gain, then claim, clarity on direction, then be creative and daring with the solutions to solve it.

As with every problem, we must first acknowledge its existence before we can move forward.

It all starts with being honest about exactly where you are. Where you really want to go—and whether your actions are truly getting you to where you want to go.

❖ Practical Section: Recognising and resetting the pull of the grind goblin

Here are the signs to help you realise when the grind goblins have gotten a hold of you and how to reset.

One:

When you start feeling the stress strings to be tight. You get restless and feel like you have to do something. Requests for time from loved ones and friends feel like weights of expectations, making you feel stressed, anxious.

When this happens—take a beat and lean into that feeling. This is the moment to listen to yourself. What is that feeling telling you? Very likely it is that you have not taken enough time for yourself, or for meeting your basic needs.

Meaning that your container of patience and space to take care of the needs of others has shrunk to the point that you have nothing to give.

Two:

When you feel overwhelmed because you realise you won't have the capacity, time, or energy to do something you truly need.

When this happens, it is a sign that you have said yes to something you probably should have said no to. And you probably need to recognise and give yourself the permission, space, and time to feel what you feel. Take a beat.

Three:

When life inevitably takes over and the crash happens. Coming back from this is threefold:

1. Carve out a few 'blackout' weekends (days with no external, work, or social plans) so you can give yourself adequate time to recover.

2. Design deliberate space in your life—especially if you have dependents (young children, elderly parents, pets).

3. Bring in something small and simple that you can keep relatively consistent to help maintain your natural centre point within yourself, whether that is a short morning meditation, a quick daily walk, or a workout.

Be non-negotiable about the time carved out for the above.

Be truthful and firm when explaining your unavailability, but don't feel like you have to make an excuse to justify why you don't have time.

These are important practices (even if initially people don't like it, because they are used to your availability) to reset boundaries.

And the most important relationships in your life will always survive this, becoming stronger because of more balanced and healthier respect for these boundaries.

> ***Exercise: Grounding to overcome the urge to grind***
>
> The urge to grind almost always stems from an external stressor.
>
> Putting things down on paper is one of the best ways to get them out of your head, gain perspective, and make it all much less overwhelming to deal with.
>
> 1. **Drill down into the real problem—what is at the root of the stress that you need to solve?**
>
> 2. **Address that.**
>
> If it's a looming deadline for a client—either put aside the time to get it done and out of the way, or evaluate whether it is actually not realistic and reset expectations.

   ANGELA TSAI

If it's a lack of time to meet commitments you have made, then evaluate if all those commitments are must-do's... or did you say yes just to be nice? Relationships are about compromise, and sometimes you are going to need to give the time—perhaps it's to help out a good friend, or something for your partner... but what are non-essential things? "I need to protect my energy this weekend" is always a polite but firm way of saying no, not making excuses. Your free time is yours to spend—filling those tubes. It is not automatically someone else's time to take.

If it's money stress—get creative. There are a million ways for you to get money. Sometimes if it requires taking on a temporary role or job, then that is what you need to do.

Note most of the 'problems' I'm highlighting here are to do with time or money; these are the external factors that mostly make us feel out of control. And these are also the external factors that often make us feel limited in being able to address the internal factors—belief that a certain path will work, or trust in yourself.

3. **Ask yourself: What would you enjoy doing right now if nothing was forced?**

What could go wrong if you don't do this right now? Can you live with that? If you've got to get it done, then do it, but commit to dedicating a specific time to something that you will truly get joy from, and lock that in.

❖ From grind to following the path to joy

Letting go of the grind was the singularly most defining moment and decision in our own business.

Our decision that we only wanted to work 16 hours a week happened in May 2022 when my daughter was 4 months old. I realised, simply, I didn't want that life anymore. The difference was that we now had the freedom to decide it, and to anchor everything around it.

What created the space was that my business partner and best friend, Cristina, also became a mother one year later. We had that space to wrap motherhood around the business fully, entirely, without sacrifice. Creating the lifestyle we wanted first, before determining what the business would look like.

And that is the reality that I want to share is possible for you as well.

The next chapters will be dedicated to painting that picture of what is possible and guiding your own reflections towards that.

PART THREE

THE PATH FORWARD

9

UNCOVER YOUR FULL POTENTIAL THROUGH VISION

The beginning of all processes with true meaning is an internal one. And the path to draw it out is not always obvious. But uncovering this is the true path to your unlimited expansion and potential.

❖ **The beginning of your path—uncovering your own vision**

To find space for our potential and unique impact, we first must create space for our true inner selves to thrive.

Away from the shadows and influences of strong, loud, opinionated voices outside.

To be ready for an outside challenge, one must first feel secure in trusting themselves.

This is the foundation of our work: helping clients nurture their self-'seeing', self-trusting, and self-direction at a deep, fundamental level.

Early stage ideas and thoughts are vulnerable and fragile on their feet. And while challenge has a crucial place, if one is not ready—it can shatter the fragile confidence and belief in self-agency in an instant.

The beginning of this process is an internal one, and the path to draw it out is not always immediate. It is a process and methodology I have simply called the 'One-Page Vision'.

❖ The One-Page Vision

The origin of the One-Page Vision was accidental.

"I want to do this… and there's this, and this…"

"Argh… I just need to find the name. The hook."

I was in a working session with my new client, Adina, mapping out the plan for a campaign we were about to launch to promote her new coaching programme.

We had met and gotten to know each other during a business retreat in Bali. She wanted to work with me, mostly because she was overwhelmed.

She was a single mum raising her three-year old. The CEO of an established social enterprise. Working part-time in corporate while writing and performing in theatre. All the while launching her brand-new coaching business.

As we were working on developing the angle of her campaign, something was feeling off. Something just wasn't clicking. Everything that we were discussing… it all felt too surface level.

There was something deeper, but the traditional line of marketing enquiry wasn't bringing it out. How did this all even connect together? Were they really separate? Who WAS Adina in all this? What was she actually selling?

And was this even the right piece to start with in the first place?

All of the above probably sounds very abstract. But that's because, in fact, it was.

We are often uncomfortable with ambiguity. It means we are quick to want to lock something down. Into a product. A package. A name. So often, people jump into business and immediately start creating websites and business cards without understanding the essence of what they are really doing and why.

Without really thinking, I pulled up a blank sheet. A sort of virtual whiteboard.

I was pulling out the words as she was talking—reflecting back to her what was formulating—her emotions, the emphasis, the words talking around 'it'.

It was a sort of live breaking down as I was literally processing and making sense of things myself. Understanding and re-conceptualising how all the abstract comes together.

What are we really selling here? How does this all connect at a deeper level?

As the structure visually took form, a sort of vision appeared. Just blocks, squares and triangles. At least that's how it felt at the time.

But what was important is that it created the space to allow us to probe, go deeper, distil. Reach clarity. Until I said, "Do you see now, how this all connects?"

It was far from a perfect picture. In fact, it looked pretty messy. It was also the very first iteration of a process that has taken place a thousand times since in sessions with clients.

It was also my first personal moment of awareness regarding what my inner diamond actually is.

Afterwards, she left me a voice message: "Angela, that thing you did— with the boxes and squares… that was amazing… I just wanted to tell you. I thought I should let you know where your special gift is."

Awareness of our inner gifts will almost always come unexpectedly and in the moments when you don't know you are in action. They are the things you most take for granted and don't acknowledge because they come naturally to you.

The answer will have been coming to you already, early in and throughout your career journey. The question is: Have you been dismissing it? Have you been open to hearing it?

❖ Practical Section: Pulling out your unique vision

The vision is always the first step—a moment of clear seeing and organising just what is in your head in this moment.

Let's face it, our minds are often a jumble of brain dumps that, over time, intertwine into a tangled web of ideas and thoughts. The essence of uniqueness will come through the small moments that initially seem insignificant. Small actions. Moments of leaning into your own intuition. Something you feel—something so strong that when you let yourself quiet down and just lean into the chaos, and just 'do', the feeling of 'alignment' suddenly falls into place.

What does the vision look like for you?

Where and who are you in all this? What is truly YOU versus what others have told you to be?

And where is the heart of it all?

Your vision, when done right, is something that remains true, no matter what changes or happens externally.

A story to illustrate:

Talia was a young client of ours. Her boyfriend was a successful self-made entrepreneur that had built his luxury export business into a small empire. Despite his attempts to help her with her business, he felt she was getting lost in her own creativity without being able to realise her ideas tangibly into business.

He loved her for her passion and believed in her potential, but his opinions and attempts to 'help' were only putting strain on their relationship. With so much success around her and the stronger voice of her boyfriend telling her who she was and what her business should be, Talia's self-doubt only worsened.

Though well-intentioned, excessive 'care and help', especially if coming from a place of "I know better" or saviour tendencies, rarely bring out real potential, which needs space to emerge from within.

What Talia really needed was for someone to just listen. To deeply nurture the ideas out. To help her shape them, and strengthen them.

To challenge her, but with a gentle hand so that she could trust herself to stand up to external scrutiny on the viability of her business ideas.

When we finally extracted her vision and found the words—captured in a clear statement—I felt the sense of relief washing over her.

Afterwards, she sent me a voice note: "Thank you… for seeing me."

It took me a couple of years to fully understand what that voice note really meant. We all need someone to fully see us while giving us the space to fully flourish into our full potential.

Exercise: Create your One-Page Vision

There are common threads that run through everything that you have done in your life up until now.

But if you don't pull this out and lay it out in a structured way, you either stay in the dream—or stay in the weeds of implementation or overwhelm. Both keep you stuck and unable to move forward. In looking back, you'll find that all the patterns have always continued to

   ANGELA TSAI

be affirming and come back to the same thing.

And personally, I am forever thankful for that early voice note from my client—that moment of seeing which nudged me down the path of discovering and owning my own gift.

Here is how to start your own journey—to self-reflect and uncover your own vision.

On a blank page, draw a line vertically about two-thirds of the way on the page. On the left side are your current and mid-term (say five years from now) areas of focus. On the right are your long-term goals (maybe 10 years from now).

Map everything out.

Look across the columns and search for the common thread… there is something there.

A note on how to handle lack of clarity or confusion

It is normal to have a lack of clarity or confusion in the early stages of discovering this.

I've noticed that people who have the fastest results are those that have a clear view of their mission and purpose in life. But this isn't something that comes overnight.

You will notice that as you continue to explore, it will keep coming back to the centre—to your core reason why you made certain decisions and choices—to leave a previous life, or step into a new one.

Try to pinpoint something that is at the heart of now. What has showed up in every aspect of your career until now? What have people loved and appreciated about you? What drives you? What would that perfect world look like (knowing that you will likely never get to the final destination, but you can move towards it)?

Exploration and engagement overcome lack of clarity or confusion. Once you've got this down, review it against the blocks you had identified to find links. Is there anything that should go because it no longer serves your full purpose?

10

WRITING YOUR VISION STATEMENT

The power of a vision statement is in that deep feeling of resonance. An anchor. A North Star. An internal feeling of safety, certainty, security, and a deep belief that no matter how you proceed, you will ultimately end up where you desire to be.

"Anything that you can imagine, you can create."—Oprah Winfrey

❖ The power of a vision statement

Tony Robbins teaches a powerful visualisation exercise that perfectly demonstrates the power of visualisation. If you only reach for a certain level, you will only get there. But if you aim for something out of reach, you will certainly go farther than you initially thought possible.

Have a go.

Twist your body as far as you can go.

Now close your eyes and envision yourself twisting all the way, like 360 degrees. Feel it.

Now do the same exercise again.

So okay, while you probably didn't snap your body (hopefully) through a full twist, you surely went further than the first 'realistic' attempt.

This is the power of having a concrete vision and a statement that powers you forward. Something that wakes you up, makes you alive.

It reminds you constantly of the WHY of what you are going for. It makes that effort so much more meaningful if that's what you choose to do. The power of a vision and mission statement delivers you more than just direction and purpose. It creates the starting point for FREEDOM.

❖ **Simplicity is the real courage to turn big dreams into reality**

Clarity is scary, as is focus. It means saying yes to one thing, and usually no to about a thousand other things. Making the first step towards pursuing your vision is already huge. It's another big step to actually commit to it.

There is romanticism in staying vague. It keeps the dream alive. It's like a safety net when you say, "It's there, I'm working on it." But it also keeps it exactly that—a dream.

Getting specific in that first step takes courage.

Crafting your vision statement serves as the foundation, to be able to choose what that right first step needs to be.

We tend to overcomplicate the first step and think it needs to be some big, magnificent thing. Much like our big visions. Gucci began in the 1930s by making saddles for the wealthy. They later expanded into other leather goods and continued to grow into a fashion empire from there.

A couple years ago, I was having coffee with a friend who was considering launching a new business venture. He was a former general manager with decades of experience in operations and people leadership. He shared that most business owners struggle with being their own general managers. I loved that insight. His proposition promised a transformation. But starting with what? Did his clients recognise that need? Did they value it enough? What was the first step for them to see and embrace the transformation?

Over the years we have seen beautiful business ideas, with incredible intention behind them, fall flat on the closed ears of the market. Because the market wasn't listening. People hadn't recognised the need.

Passions die, and bitterness takes their place.

We underestimate the power of simplicity in the first step. The

simpler the better.

The first step is relatable. The first step is simple. The first step is accessible. The first step is needed now. That is what you want your first step to feel like to your potential customers.

The clearer it is—acting as the wedge in an almost completely closed door—the more it unlocks openness towards a broader transformation.

❖ Choosing the first step of the big dream

The first step is both the hardest and the easiest. It is easy to dive straight in, but at the same time it's hard—because you need to pick a beginning point. Rather than simply follow the current of the river, you need to know where to dive in. Which may feel like you are holding back.

The criteria shift as you start to build and your needs begin to shift.

Maslow's hierarchy illustrates that we must satisfy lower-level basic needs before we can address higher-level growth needs. In order to fulfil your total mission and potential, you need to establish a solid foundation first upon which to build. You need to ensure your basic needs are met—such as financial stability and alignment with your values—before progressing to higher levels of growth and development.

In other words, you need to fully monetise your initial steps while staying true to your mission before expanding further.

The goal of the vision statement is to provide a singular anchor around your entire mission. Crafting it takes effort because of its importance—but also, you shouldn't feel stuck here, as this statement will certainly be tuned and refined.

The right vision statement for you will hold a certain emotional weight.

It will feel aligned energy-wise. It will feel like YOUR voice. Not anyone else's. It should inspire and create a level of discomfort, but not feel so ridiculously out of reach and lofty that it makes you feel it is unattainable for you—or that it is, in fact, someone else's vision.

This is because the vision statement will continue to be a living component of your business as you live your vision, as you play, as it continues to resonate and grow roots in your heart and mind. And you will refine it as you continue to level up and shift your identity.

But the key here is you must be able to visualise it.

Stretching yourself just beyond what you can visualise normally, then adding on another 50%, pushes you beyond your comfort. It provides inspiration, but doesn't shut down your brain.

Exercise: Craft your vision statement

1. Go back to the final exercise from the last chapter. Review again your One-Page Vision, and look for a common thread that runs throughout.

2. Try to craft your vision statement. What are the key words that emphasise the feeling and energy that need to be there?

3. Don't worry about envisioning this as a headline or tagline. This vision statement is not for others to see. This is a private beacon of inspiration, a North Star, to help you continuously re-anchor to yourself and come back on.

❖ Common hurdles when it comes to vision statements

Here are 4 common hurdles that often come up when I run through this exercise with clients (and what to do about them):

1. Feeling blocked from finding the words to articulate your feelings and visions.

Diego was a freelance web designer that wanted to pivot to his real passion for coaching and mentoring others. His biggest challenge was distilling the essence of his offering in a way that didn't sound generic. The small business / coaching market is crowded, and only continuing to become more so with low barriers to entry. It thus becomes difficult to discern the real deal from those selling surface-level knowledge lifted off the latest YouTube video without the depth of real experience.

Yet, there is no-one out there that is meant to do and deliver exactly what you do, in the unique way you do it.

In Diego's case, as we began to explore his vision together more deeply, he realised that the power behind his message wasn't just in the words—it was in the authenticity and energy that came from his own lived experiences. The more he connected to his core 'why' and what made him come alive, the clearer his message became. By simplifying his approach and focusing on the key actions and impact he wanted to deliver, Diego was able to create a vision that resonated with both himself and his future clients.

In other words—your unique experiences and authenticity are what truly set you apart and are what you actually bring into your business.

The words are one thing, but it's about the energy behind them that will come as your confidence grows. You will likely find that the more experience you build, the more you re-anchor back to simplicity.

But in the beginning, getting at the heart and essence of what you do, and why you do it, and why you do it so uniquely, is core. It gives you the clarity and anchor, as the words are then moulded around it, to feel out what feels authentic and true and what doesn't.

> **Your turn: Start with pinpointing the key words that need to be present. What makes you feel alive? What action words need to be present? What words represent the unique impact you want to make?**

2. **The statement is too convoluted or long and you're unable to cut it down.**

Simplifying and distilling is hard. It's again about making choices.

Sometimes in our attempt to say more, squeeze in more words, we end up saying nothing at all.

Jonathan was a pharmaceuticals executive who became a freelance consultant and trainer. He worked in quality assurance, and his passion for this was ignited while seeing his wife go through cancer treatment. It allowed the hard reality of the end impact on the patient, at the end of these long clinical studies and manufacturing lines of drugs, to hit home.

Quality controls and processes were not a matter of just doing a job, nor were the various functions and departments within the pharmaceutical company. They had very real impact, even in their small contribution towards ultimately potentially saving someone's life.

It became Jonathan's passion to awaken this realisation within the workforce and young entrants into the pharmaceutical industry, to help them see this as something beyond simply a job.

With his decades of experience and what he accumulated, it took us several sessions to narrow down this vision statement to something that fully captured the heart—while also being selective and taking out what was merely supportive so we could fully emphasise and focus on what needed to be highlighted in the forefront, identifying his driving force of energy.

In your vision statement, the process here is about refinement.

Your turn: Have a go at the initial version. Focus on those initial words that capture the right feeling, tone, and energy. Make sure certain words that NEED to be there are there.

3.   You're being too narrow or not thinking big enough.

I have found that those with the most experience often struggle the most with creating expansive vision statements.

Experiences humble us. And when we are accustomed to being just one part of the bigger wheel, and have been clobbered into thinking that we simply need to get in line, it's difficult to break out of that to start thinking big. We are trained to think in measurables, and fear our inability to hold up to a promise.

This was especially the case with Michelle, an award-winning marketing superstar, backed by decades of experience, but who feared claiming something that felt beyond her.

This is also a common challenge, from what we have seen, with clients that have come from marketing, creative, and strategic branding backgrounds. They mix up a vision statement with a brand promise, or a tagline for their product. This isn't it. This is a narrow container that sits underneath something much broader.

The North Star.

A vision statement needs to give you the feeling of energy, of excitement—and an awareness that it may fit the container for your entire life… not just the next two to three years.

4.   The statement doesn't feel like it's yours.

Comparison is the thief of joy. This is the feeling when your vision statement feels like it's borrowed from others.

And this is often due to early outside exposure to our fragile ideas and initial spark—being told, being pushed, being challenged before we were ready. It triggers us to build up defensive walls to meet those critiques too quickly, before we've cemented the strength from within.

The greatness is already inside you, and waiting to be pulled out. External statements and what others tell you that you should be can often come at the risk of further suppressing that inner unique spark, which requires a quiet nurturing to pull out.

I experienced this in the process of finding my feet in my own vision. I noticed my own triggers and feelings of inadequacy or of being not enough when hearing about someone else's vision. Should it be more?

I leaned into that feeling. What was going on here? And created another version, of course… something that felt 'bigger'.

But that also didn't feel right. To be even more specific, it felt like I was wearing someone else's pants that didn't quite fit.

Look out for the feeling of inadequacy. Perhaps when you heard or saw something from someone else, that's when you started to compare.

ANGELA TSAI

Look out for the feeling of inauthenticity. Perhaps you felt like your vision needed to be more.

Creating from this place will push you into a space where you are crafting a vision statement to be impressive to someone else rather than it truly coming from you.

This is about it becoming undeniably yours, without the pressure or expectation to be like someone else.

Your turn: The process I guide clients through is a deep one of self-enquiry and mirror reflecting-back statements.

Throwing something back. Tasting how it feels. Playing with it in the space. Perhaps sometimes putting something provocative out there, just to see how it feels, if there is room to stretch.

In absence of this, my recommendation is to ask those closest to you, those you trust, a simple question: "What do you believe is unique or special about me?"

Write their statements down. Take the time to absorb the statements and feel out what the essence is.

What resonates with you? This is likely at the core of something inside you, that you know innately to be true.

What feels like a mask? These are likely aspects that are a part of you, but are not the core. You pull this out mostly for the benefit of appeasing or creating some sort of impression on others.

Ask yourself again: What is a key word that signifies your life theme?

Then come back again to your vision statement.

11

STAYING FOCUSED THROUGH ECONOMICS AND NUMBERS

· · ● · · —

"There's not enough time to do all the things you DON'T want to do."

—*Gay Hendricks, The Big Leap*

❖ **Feasible versus fantasy**

I was sitting in a cafe, incredibly nervous. I had a folder with printed pages sitting neatly on the table next to my matcha latte, ready to meet my new potential client. A glass jug of water sat beside it, already half empty as I drank water to calm my nerves and what felt like a ridiculously dry throat that wouldn't go away.

This wasn't someone that should have been intimidating, at least to me. It was one of my closest friends that I have known for years.

The nervousness came not because I was unsure how she was going to take the news I was about to share or whether that would affect her trust to work with me.

I had run the numbers based on the revenue and business goals she shared, creating a campaign to drive the 1:1 discovery conversations to grow her coaching business. I wanted to show her that this approach wasn't feasible and would become a full-time job to meet her revenue targets with the current parameters.

Presenting the business case this way fundamentally changed the campaign's direction.

We shifted to a group coaching program sold via webinars, based on the economics and the effort required for 90-minute discovery sessions.

That awareness teamed with the focused approach resulted in a fully sold-out first programme launch.

But the key takeaway is this: the best results come from starting with a clear, focused strategy that's grounded in the numbers. By taking a data-driven, numbers approach, it provides the parameters to rethink your approach to achieve success.

It is the difference between struggling with unrealistic goals, vs. facing reality, pivoting and actually thriving.

❖ **Practical Section: Making decisions through numbers (your business case scenarios)**

Numbers create clarity. They create focus. They make what feels like an impossibility around your goals achievable because numbers break things down into inputs. They are also the ultimate vetter in that decision-making process of choosing the first step.

One of my favourite definitions of economics is by Russ Roberts—that economics is basically a study of choice under constraints.

Knowing your numbers in business provides you with exactly the inputs and considerations needed to make that choice. And there is no right or wrong choice, only what is going to be most aligned with your intentions and where you want to go.

Running numbers on the desired business case scenario my client was looking to build showed the outcome and what was required for it to add up—thereby giving us clarity to pivot.

Exercise: Working out your own economics and numbers

Now let's have a look at your own numbers. There are only a few simple key numbers you must know:

1. **Revenue goals** – I recommend mapping this out onto three levels:

   - Personal subsistence (what you need as a baseline to be comfortable)

   - Ideal lifestyle (what you want ideally)

- Bigger vision

2. Calculable units

- How your product/service is (currently) packaged and unit prices

Don't worry if this is not fully set or exact just yet. It is simply a means to model and project possibilities so that you can make decisions based on recognition of the energy that is needed to go into it.

3. Capacity

- How many hours you are happy to work

This is an important one.

4. Current conversion baselines

- Conversions on qualified people at this moment (if you have any)

Playing with these numbers provides you with the basis to model scenarios and, more importantly, overlay whether or not a scenario is in line with the business you are envisioning and whether you will be happy within that scenario.

12

AWAKEN YOUR REAL INNER EXTRAORDINARINESS (YOUR INNER DIAMOND)

— • ● • —

"Don't ask what the world needs. Ask what makes you come alive, and go do it. Because what the world needs is people who have come alive."

- Howard Thurman

❖ **What you are not meant for**

Most of us are conditioned (unintentionally) early on in our lives not to dream. We are taught to be realistic, not to be 'ridiculous', and to honour responsibilities over passions.

The trouble is, when children hear the words "Don't be ridiculous" or "Don't be silly", no matter how trivially it is said, it starts to become ingrained in them and they start to believe it. That voice permeates into every part of their lives—unless we realise and awaken from it.

So, if something is in you, fighting, and knowing that there is more to you, then there is.

My hands were shaking, my heart was beating; I had been practicing for hours every day for the last three months leading up to this moment.

I stepped up on the stage of the piano competition hall and walked up to the grand piano.

As my fingers danced across the keys, I fumbled, and I could hear my notes slip. My fingers were stiff from nervousness and the winter cold.

I recalled in that instant seeing another girl holding a hot water bottle with her hands wrapped in towels, and now I understood why. I was devastated. I blurred my way through the piece and rushed off the stage to scattered clapping. I blew it.

To be honest, I don't really recall what my mum or piano teacher might have said to me after that—I'm not sure I would have taken it in. I'm sure they said something like, "Oh well, you did your best, try again next time." But I believe deep down, I'd already decided there wasn't going to be a next time.

When we decide to stay small, to stay average, that's where we stay.

I knew that wasn't good enough, but the energy followed me into corporate. As I continued to ascend with that constant push and drive like a fire within me, I always told myself not to look forward to the promotion in case it didn't happen.

Looking back, what that day in the piano competition hall taught me (wrongly) was a fear of seeking feedback.

I simply stopped asking for it. Not because of a confidence that I didn't need the validation, which would have been healthier, but out of a fear of invalidation and rejection.

I pursued my goals relentlessly, anchoring my sense of inner worth and confidence on external milestones only. The speed of promotions. The speed of deliverables. The speed of getting hard outcomes and delivering.

But when someone tells you that you are not meant for something, and it awakens a fire in you—then that is a sign.

A calling to step up, to defend and claim your place on the throne of your inner worth.

For me, that was when a group director told me, as I sought his advice and feedback on my next progression, that he saw me as someone not laying the path, but running it. Calmly, I absorbed this and nodded my head—with a furiousness inside that told me there wasn't a single truth in what he said.

How much longer are we willing to accept the limits that others set on us, based on the limited view that they have seen, and that we have allowed ourselves to believe?

❖ Awakening your inner diamond

Your own awakening will occur when you are ready to receive it.

And you will be enlightened to your most valuable gifts by those around you—someone outside of you. But you need to be open in order to see or hear it. It may take several times of hearing it from multiple perspectives and places, and of you being in a sufficient place of "I'm fed up with this", to be ready to claim it.

Strength and your unique value come from one source, and that is owning and fully claiming who you truly are…

…then stepping into that.

When I first entered the business world, it was a natural step to dive straight into consulting, working freelance and contracting for people that I already knew. It was a mentoring session with one of my early mentors—a powerhouse woman—that shook me awake.

"The name you have chosen," she said—Grow Your Brand With Impact—"it's like it has space for infinite growth. But you have just taken one small corner."

Damn, I realised. She was totally right.

She challenged me. "Tell me again what you do."

I blurted out, "I am the founder of Grow Your Brand With Impact, and my mission is to be the owner of global business schools supporting and empowering women."

   ANGELA TSAI

My vision has since evolved, but I'll always be grateful for those early moments of awakening and a pull to think bigger.

What we need to remember is that people value and will perceive different aspects of you for a reason relevant to themselves. They are drawn to you for a reason. There is a piece of you that connects with a piece of who they are themselves.

But it is hard to see, because we have lived our entire lives in the shadow of other people's projections, expectations, and external mirrors telling us what they see.

There's a story of a young woman who was in a fight at a bar; she was pushed onto the floor and suffered a head trauma and woke up not remembering anything about herself.

She had lost her container for long-term memories and was suddenly waking up in a hospital room with several people at her bedside, and she had no idea who they were. One identified herself as her mother, another her best friend, another her sister, and another her boyfriend. "Can you tell me about who I am? And what happened to me?" Each told a very different story, but especially about aspects of her personality and what they believed, saw., or interpreted would have happened that night.

Our identity for large parts of our lives has been framed through outside labels—job titles, degrees and certifications, salary levels, and 'roles'. We have lost touch with being able to see ourselves from within, who we truly are without all those things, and the real essence of the value that has always existed within.

It's like the vines that exist in rainforests. They are wrapped around magnificent trees reaching for the skies… so much so, they almost become part of the tree. Yet they are separate. They are not the tree. They form, in fact, a very important part of maintaining the ecosystem as part of the regeneration process, whilst providing a 'highway' for the animals that live within the rainforest.

The problem is that we are often simply too close to our situation to see the woods for the trees—to see what is really important, valuable, and should be placed front and centre.

❖ Stripping out the noise to focus on your real value

Steve Jobs once famously said: "People think focus is about saying yes to the thing you've got to focus on. But that's not what it means at all. It means saying no to the hundred other good ideas that there are. You have to pick carefully."

There have been multiple times in our business journey when I was tempted to spread out once more. I knew we had the potential, the knowledge. We just needed to package it up and start selling it. But was it the right thing to do?

The business started like that—expanding with no limit. The team were ambitious and driven. Clients kept wanting more from us, and we were readily stepping up each time. But what resulted was an expanding team, spread completely thin and burning oil at all the ends.

Becoming a specialist does not limit who you become, but it allows you to go deeper and make even more impact.

If you peel down enough layers of the onion and discover what that is—uniquely for you—we call that the inner diamond. You will discover that it is, in fact, the piece that has allowed you to amplify your impact in everything else that you have done since then.

13

EMOTIONAL TOOLS & MINDSET TO EXECUTE ON YOUR INNER DIAMOND… WITHOUT THE BURNOUT

"Most prefer to simply dream about the life they could have had, rather than believing in ourselves enough to embody such a life. And the reason is fear."

—Richard Rudd, *The Gene Keys*

❖ **Showing up authentically**

I'm sitting in a cafe. It's tired-looking, but with a spark of… something. It would have felt nondescript apart from the corner wall that suddenly caught my attention.

A panel on the wall with a bunch of random stickers—rock and roll, art, and punk. The Wi-Fi code was MaitaiWaikiki, with a wall of postcards in the corner. These were the only flashes of personality, as the rest of the cafe felt boring and plain.

There were other elements with promise. The bronze-plated undercounter. The deliberately industrial-looking lamps. Antique leather stools. But it was almost like someone just said… okay, that's good enough. And let it be. It felt like an empty bedroom long abandoned by a lively teenager and since replaced with other things that needed to use the space. The panel became a wall of nostalgia hidden in the corner, long forgotten.

It made me wonder about the full flair of the person who owned the cafe and implemented these splashes. Where did the vision begin? Was it meant to be alternative, or the generic 'safe' decor that it became, which felt more appeasing to the masses?

It was a few short months later that I walked past the same cafe and a repossession sign was stuck over the door. They ran out of steam.

It made me think of how often we go through life and live. Especially in pursuit of our dreams.

Instead of showing the full flair of who we are, and going after it—we suppress and adapt what we have to offer and how we express it, to become more acceptable. More appealing to the masses.

We all know people in our lives that seem to show up more loudly and put themselves on display more than others. Yet this doesn't always mean showing up authentically, as it's often a performance. And those

    ANGELA TSAI

whose full expression does not come out unless in the quiet intimacy of those that know them best. Perhaps that is you?

What I have learnt is that if you get to know and dig around someone long enough, you will eventually discover an absolutely fascinating person. Most people simply don't have the patience to dig. Or get so blinded by the 'in-your-face' loud personalities that the real essence fades into the background.

When did we forget how to show up authentically (and vulnerably) as ourselves?

What's important is that the interesting and fascinating person is within all of us. Most of us have just forgotten that that person is there. We have become accustomed to hiding them, pushing them down into more socially acceptable moulds. More attention-grabbing moulds, or 'proper' ways of being.

We have forgotten how it feels to let who we truly are shine.

Somewhere in the journey of life, we have learnt that it is unsafe or less desirable to be ourselves, to the extent that we have begun to suppress our full selves, and started living for others' approval.

❖ Practical Section: Rediscovering your authenticity

Being authentic and true to who you are, with vulnerability, means allowing yourself to be.

Loving yourself fully as you are, and allowing that expression of imperfection to be seen. Being you for you, and not for the approval of anyone else. Trusting yourself at your core that you are already good.

Suppressing the negative aspects of yourself will also mean suppressing the good because these are what has festered in the darkness and grown, due to an open wound. They are as much a part of you as the positive parts we put out into the world. To fully accept the darkness is to heal. And this is part of the true, authentic expression of you.

Now, over to you—how authentically are you currently showing up in each area of your life? What masks, if any, might you be wearing—to prevent hurting others, to prevent losing approval, to prevent 'stepping on toes'? How would you show up if you were being fully _you_?

Exercise: Running your own authenticity test

Take a scan across the key areas in your life where you spend time right now:

- With your partner

- With your family

- With your friends

- During work

- When you are alone

- When interacting with your broader network and the public stage (including social media)

Write down what your view of being fully authentic and vulnerable would mean for each of these areas.

Score yourself out of 10 in terms of your ability to feel vulnerable and safe to authentically express yourself.

Ask yourself the following questions:

1. What mask, if any, am I wearing? ("I am being inauthentic because… I am pretending that… when in fact…")

2. What is the trigger for something to feel off in this area?

3. How would I show up if I was being fully me? What is the fear that comes up when I envision myself doing that?

❖ **Setting & enforcing personal boundaries**

Boundaries are the respect of the relationship you have with yourself.

Without them in place, no healthy relationships can flourish, nor can you achieve your full potential.

The thing we often fight hardest to protect is the thing we most risk losing through not being ourselves. This realisation is the starting point to owning who we are and showing up authentically (and vulnerably).

We all have this experience in our relationships. Moments when we have to decide whether to stay silent and act 'fine' or speak up and risk confrontation.

This is especially true for relationships where we don't have everyday contact.

Perhaps because we want to enjoy the limited time we do spend together, we don't want to make those interactions uncomfortable. Or perhaps we feel insecure about the stability of those relationships when we don't see them every day.

However, your ability to show up authentically and set healthy boundaries is what is needed to deepen the relationship and allow someone to truly see you. Even in your most vulnerable and imperfect moments.

Without honesty, friendships rely on superficial interactions, social media likes, and empty platitudes. The slightest disruption can destroy these relationships, and being overly accommodating sets false expectations, leading to resentment on both sides.

I have personally found that addressing the dynamics of my relationships, the core of where my most intimate authenticity shows up, was the beginning step to help me open up authenticity everywhere else.

❖ Build up real confidence from within

Real confidence starts with boundaries. It takes confidence firstly to know your personal boundaries and come to terms with them.

This means recognising what you are losing when you don't honour them. Learning to fully listen to yourself with your heart. And creating the courage to say no.

You'll know when you have it—that feeling of real confidence from within—when you get a sense of the depth of real relaxation. You are simply sure of yourself and in your skin.

We often mistake lack of confidence for lack of 'competence'. They are not the same things.

Confidence will naturally come through a build-up of competence. Competence is simply a boundary we have at this moment that we are working on stretching.

And the certainty is knowing that through this journey, you will build competence. Gain the results. Receive validation, and all the things that will continue to strengthen that external confidence—things that are visible, and that others see as success and assurance.

But it all begins from within. The self-certainty and groundedness that drive inner confidence. This is the difference between confidence that is projected (outer only) versus radiated (inner confidence).

The graph below illustrates this development.

Build Up Real Confidence From Within

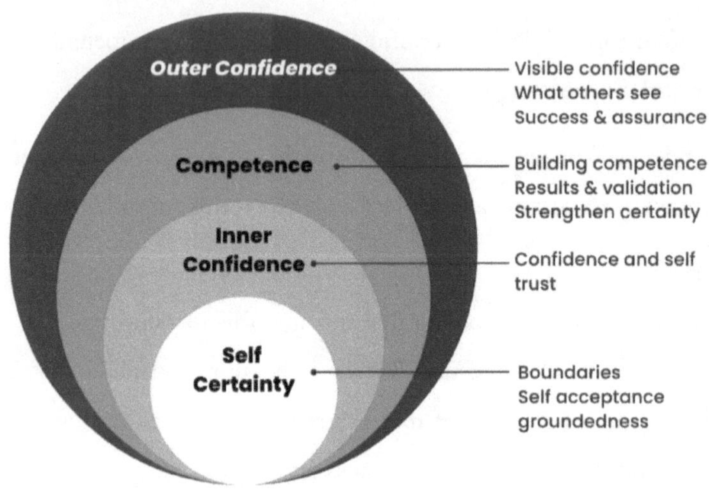

❖ **Stages of showing up**

Ever notice that the moments that real confidence and competence show up are often the moments where you have no opportunity at all to think?

It was the first webinar I delivered postpartum, at about four weeks after giving birth. I was sleep deprived, running back and forth daily to the hospital's Neonatal Intensive Care ward to visit and deliver pumped milk for my daughter. And it was probably one of the best I'd ever delivered up until that point.

Often we are in flow simply because we have no other choice. No time for our overthinking brain to kick in. We are simply acting and responding to the moment.

I was in flow that morning simply because I had no other choice.

Imagine the relaxed conversation when you are in the semi-dark at a campsite, tired and happy after a long hike. Or perhaps speaking with your friends in the dark as a child at a sleepover.

There is something about the dim lights that takes away the cover of who we are in daylight—in our roles to perform as an entrepreneur, employee, leader…

The real flow of showing up comes when you are able to bring that state of relaxation even in the moments when you need to 'perform'.

The five stages

There are five core stages when it comes to re-learning and connecting with your authenticity and showing up.

1) The mask – performing (you are showing up for someone else). This first stage is often the one in which we are most unaware. It is the one we are the most accustomed to living in, because we have almost always been performing for someone else's approval or validation.

Here are the signs that you're wearing the mask:

- You frequently speak about positive achievements over real struggles.

- When someone asks how you are, you automatically respond with "Great!" or something along those lines.

- You thrive on validation—social media likes and comments—and feel triggered to take action when you don't get the validation.

- You find yourself seeking validation through others' approval and opinions.

Positivity and hope are good things—having them is a superpower. But vulnerability makes them real. It makes them believable. It is dynamite. The buffeting between is a normal ebb and flow.

Nobody believes that everyone's got it figured out.

Once a week, sit down and write down the things you really struggled with. It could be in the areas of relationship dynamics, work, your children, or a personal struggle you faced. Reflect on the moments of negative emotion and capture those.

Consider sharing those struggles in your stories.

2) Pain of inauthenticity – something feels off. At this point, something will start to feel disconnected. Often this comes down to a sense of shame, or fear of critique and judgment. Sometimes we even place this on ourselves, through our inner critic voice.

There is a conflicting energy of wanting to show up, but not knowing how. A constant state of feeling like people don't really see you for the real you.

3) Fear – realisation of the deep fear ("What if people see me and don't really like me?"). Acknowledging this gap is the beginning of opening up.

This stage is the recognition of the inner dialogue and the voices that are running within. It shines a light on the real hurdles that are preventing us from showing up. I talk through a lot of the strategies to overcome this in chapters 5 & 6.

4) Self-love and letting go of expectations – overcoming the inner critic (which is often where we imagine the vocalisation of external critics) begins with a lot of self-compassion.

Recognise the phase is normal. Don't beat yourself up. Don't compare yourself to others' progress. Simply accept this is where you are, with the intention to move forward.

There is no other voice that you need to be; know that you already have the natural presence within you. It's just about letting go of the external shells that have been holding it in. The mental ones. The emotional ones. And the projected expectations from others that were never our own.

5) Start to show up – with fear in your heart, but courage in your soul, do it anyway.

This is the knowledge that this fear is but a phase—an acceptance of its existence—and will only get better.

❖ **Practical Section: Owning your stories**

This book began with a theme about feeling storyless. I would be amiss to not include at least a section dedicated to this topic.

At the core of being able to show up authentically and vulnerably is the ability to open the space to dare to share your stories.

But what if we haven't learnt that our stories matter?

I've personally always experienced a block in writing out my own, and sharing them.

The story I told myself was "I don't have interesting stories rooted in deep, 'real' trauma. I haven't lost my parents at an early age. I haven't had a serious medical condition that made me appreciate the miracle and value of life to be lived to its fullest."

But the stories are there. Deeply rooted in experiences that sometimes span generations back.

Not acknowledging our personal experiences as significant, as 'enough', is the starting point of disconnection.

Exercise: Write out your most significant stories, negative and positive. What has shaped you to be who you are and to do what you are doing today?

Start from the beginning (childhood) and work your way to present day. It's a good idea to keep this as a note somewhere easy to access on your phone. Get into a habit of capturing moments, experiences, and stories throughout the day.

This exercise is working your mental muscle for noticing and capturing stories that are happening every second of the day. It is training your awareness and recognition of the significance of these stories.

We acknowledge and connect to our past through how we frame these experiences, re-learning how to connect the dots and relationships in our brain.

A first step towards being able to share them externally.

But also towards really starting to recognise the unique depth of what we bring of value to the world.

❖ Practical Section: Walking the fine balance of sharing… without shame or regret

There is a real fear that being authentic and vulnerable means oversharing. Especially in today's age of social media. How much information is too much information?

Well, my personal view is… there is no black-and-white rule. The only guiding star is your own principles and values, as well as intention.

When I started my own vulnerable process of unpacking the first edits of this book, I grounded myself on five core principles:

- Protect my family

- Protect my business partnership

- Protect my daughter and my husband

- Honour my truth and be compassionate with my feelings in this process

- Focus only on what will serve and help others

Anchoring to these meant that I had the safety to express myself, without the fear that the eventual external version will ever compromise these.

I recommend evaluating your own anchoring principles around your relationships that are most at risk because of their role in making you who you are today, and the journey you have been on.

Know this, then let go, and be assured that this safety will hold you.

> *Exercise: Anchoring your authentic expression through your unique values*
>
> 1) What must you protect?
>
> 2) What must you do to honour you?
>
> 3) What is serving the greater good or audience group that you are sharing with?
>
> 4) Lead with your heart in all the answers above.

❖ **Handling rejection and perceived failures (with acceptance and grace)**

Here's the thing with those stages in learning to show up authentically.

They are not linear. And it doesn't mean that you pass them like levels in a game. They are cyclical… and just when you start to show up, it is easy to once again start slipping back into 'the mask'.

Here's what to do when the inevitable knocks come to your 'outer confidence'—usually a sign that our inner confidence has not been

ANGELA TSAI

properly cemented.

Create Space

1. **Realise it's not only about you**: Look at the situation objectively from both your perspective and the other person's.

2. **Put it into perspective**: Ask yourself, on which side is the perceived failure? Is it really true or always true, or more of an anomaly?

Create Purpose

1. **Recognize failure as part of the journey**: Understand that failure is just another stepping stone.

2. **Find the lesson**: Instead of thinking "I'm not good enough", ask what this event is trying to teach you. It might be about boundaries, setting expectations, or something else.

Create Energy

1. **Reframe the situation**: Once you've created space and perspective, start diagnosing—what *really* happened?

2. **Move forward constructively**: Use the insights gained to help you move forward without losing the genuine confidence you've built.

Be Open

- **Embrace and practice acceptance**: Don't put up walls; lovingly create space for whatever the response may be.

❖ A final note on accountability

From my experience, everything important requires the support of accountability, and we do provide that should that be something you are seeking.

I am lucky in this way to have a business partner where we hold each other accountable, as well as coaches and guides who support the various aspects of my personal and business priorities (including the writing of this book!).

Share your vision and accountability with people you trust. People that will get excited for your vision. People you know will nudge you when you slip back into old ways.

It doesn't matter if you get off track.

What matters is the periodic review, the accountability and support structure, and knowing that the vision will be there for you to pick up once more.

14

EPILOGUE
THE UNFINISHED STORY (CREATING YOUR DREAM)

"With an adventurous heart and the right maps, we can travel anywhere and never fear losing ourselves."—*Brené Brown*

Wrapping up: The truth about dreams and daring to proceed

So much can be said about living bravely, yet it all comes down to real courage and doing it.

What would you do if you didn't need to work and make money?

Most of us stay in dream mode without taking any steps forward. Our lofty dreams keep us in a comfortable place, knowing we have potential but never moving forward.

Recognising the things that will hold you back means knowing the difference between following the current versus guiding the flow of the stream.

When we don't know who we are, and are being carried along by the current—as we often are in our careers—it is easy to lose ourselves whenever there is a fork in the river path. We'll simply go down whichever stream has the strongest current.

At the end of the day, we will all end up in the sea. The question is, was it the stream, or life, we really wanted to live?

And the real things that hold us back from going for it stem, most of the time, from within. A result of not knowing who we truly are or what we truly want, and deep, deep fear around claiming it all.

The details of the execution at that level of awareness almost become irrelevant, as the most important thing is whether you are making micro steps towards your destination.

Jumping into the Matrix: Inner clarity

One of our clients once described this process of gaining inner clarity as feeling like he's finally ready to take the red pill and jump into the Matrix.

Inner clarity is this deep work that shakes. It forces you into confrontation with your deepest resistances. The feeling of wanting to run away. The feeling of delving deep. The comfort and temptation of staying on the surface and gliding across the surface-level marketing, packaging, and messaging. The exact thing that has prevented you from getting to where you truly need to be.

Direction. Deep inner alignment. A confrontation of the truth. Who are you? What do you need? Do you really want this? And what IS 'this'?

My dream for YOU, dear reader, is that you can claim this clarity for yourself.

Thus claiming back the joy in your daily path towards the long-term vision (destination)—and if you are not currently living it, to claim the path there.

In career, in business, in love.

This book has aimed to serve as a guide to help you spend the time upfront to properly get to know who you are and what you want, then to uncover your real value and awaken it—your inner diamond.

Done right, your vision will never be a finished story.

It will continue to evolve as you continue to build out and grow. But it will never lose its core essence.

This becomes the practice of learning to start listening to your heart— tuning into the inner voice that pulls you forward, separating out the inner voices that are coming from a place of fear, guiding you constantly back to the truth of your destiny.